Praise for The Strategic Empathy Revolution

Author Loretta Piazza's **The Strategic Empathy Revolution** is a compelling invitation to personal and professional transformation.

Through her insightful narrative, Loretta challenges readers to take a bold leap, redefining leadership through empathy, reflection, and meaningful action.

At the heart of the book lies the BRIDGE Framework, a versatile and practical model designed for application across diverse sectors - from education and corporate environments to the evolving digital landscape.

Loretta doesn't shy away from asking the difficult questions - those often left unspoken in leadership discourse. She interrogates the value of authority versus understanding and makes a compelling case for why traditional leadership paradigms are no longer sufficient in today's world. Her approach encourages readers to rewire their thinking, using the BRIDGE Framework as a catalyst for deeper insight and sustainable change.

Drawing on real-world examples, including her coaching and mentoring work with Jamie, a leader in education, and Kathy, a CEO in the corporate sector, Loretta illustrates the transformative power of empathy-driven leadership. These stories are not only relatable; they're profoundly impactful.

More than a guide, **The Strategic Empathy Revolution** is a conversation waiting to be had. Loretta shows that engaging in challenging, often uncomfortable dialogue is the gateway to authentic leadership. The BRIDGE Framework becomes not just a tool, but a compass - helping readers navigate the complexities of modern leadership with clarity, confidence, and compassion.

A must-read for anyone seeking to lead with purpose and evolve with intention.

Deborah Patterson - Former Principal, Author, Mentor & Coach

THE STRATEGIC EMPATHY REVOLUTION

Building high performance teams with emotional intelligence

DR LORETTA PIAZZA

Copyright © 2025 Dr Loretta Piazza

All rights reserved. No part of this book may be used or reproduced in any form whatsoever without written permission except in the case of brief quotations in critical articles or reviews.

ISBN: 978-1-7643220-0-3

CONTENTS

INTRODUCTION: THE AUTHORITY ILLUSION 9

PART 1: ILLUMINATE 15

1: SILENT ROOMS, DEAD IDEAS: THE AUTHORITY PARADOX 16

2: THE EMPATHY REVOLUTION: WHY UNDERSTANDING OUTPERFORMS AUTHORITY ... 23

3: FROM COMMAND TO CATALYST: WHY TRADITIONAL LEADERSHIP IS DYING 34

PART 2: METAMORPHOSIS 42

4: REWIRE YOUR LEADERSHIP BRAIN: THE BRIDGE TO EXTRAORDINARY INFLUENCE 43

5: TRIGGER POINTS: MAPPING EMOTIONAL LANDMINES IN LEADERSHIP 55

6: THE LEADERSHIP MATRIX: SEE WHAT OTHERS CAN'T 67

7: THE INTEGRATION CODE: WHERE EMPATHY MEETS STRATEGY 78

8: BEYOND GOOD INTENTIONS: MAKING IT STICK 91

9: BEYOND YOUR PRESENCE: BUILDING LEADERSHIP THAT LASTS 100

10: THE SUCCESS THAT KILLS: WHY WINNING LEADERS LOSE THEIR EDGE 112

PART 3: TRANSCEND 123

11: FROM TRAINWRECK TO MASTERY: WHY DIFFICULT CONVERSATIONS MAKE OR BREAK YOU 124

12: FORGED IN FIRE: HOW CRISIS CAN MAKE A LEADER DANGEROUS 140

13: LEADING ACROSS DISTANCES: THE NEW FRONTIER FOR REMOTE LEADERSHIP 149

14: BEYOND THE BRIDGE: YOUR STRATEGIC EMPATHY REVOLUTION 157

NOTES 167

Acknowledgments 177

INTRODUCTION: THE AUTHORITY ILLUSION

Let me tell you about the moment I discovered that everything I thought I knew about leadership was completely wrong.

Whilst at the pinnacle of my career, I was seconded to a newly established Department of Education branch set up to develop principal health and wellbeing programmes. I should have been thrilled about the opportunity to make a real difference. Instead, I walked into that government office carrying something that felt like a lead weight in my chest: the raw, devastating understanding that comes from losing your best friend and colleague to suicide.

This wasn't just professional knowledge I brought to the role. This was insight paid for at the highest possible price. It's the kind of deep, painful wisdom that only comes from watching someone you care about struggle in silence until they couldn't struggle anymore.

I knew things about principal wellbeing that no research study could capture. I understood the crushing isolation, the impossible pressure, the way our systems could slowly erode even the strongest leaders.

I had solutions born from grief, strategies forged in the crucible of loss, and a fierce determination to ensure no other principal would face what my friend had faced alone.

Through this I discovered something profound about authority-based systems. They don't recognise the value of human understanding.

When wisdom meets bureaucracy

My insights crashed against the first wall almost immediately: "Do your thoughts and ideas really fit our direction?" The question came from someone who had never spent a day in a principal's office, never felt the weight of being responsible for hundreds of students and dozens of staff, never experienced the suffocating isolation that can consume school leaders.

But they had authority. They had position. They had the power to decide whose ideas mattered.

When some of my proposals finally began moving forward, after countless revisions and committee approvals, another barrier appeared: "XYZ needs to approve this." Then another: "We'll need to run this past the steering committee." And another: "This will require ministerial sign-off."

I watched my understanding get filtered through layer after layer of bureaucracy. Each approval process stripped away more of the human urgency. By the time my insights reached the decision-makers who could implement them, their essence had evaporated. The moment was gone, the opportunity squandered.

But the most heartbreaking part? While we were playing approval games, principals were still struggling. Some were still suffering in silence. The very people these programmes were meant to help were waiting for permission that might never come.

The pattern that changes everything

That experience opened my eyes to something I'd been missing throughout my entire leadership career. It's not just about missed opportunities or inefficient processes. It's watching passionate, engaged human beings transform into passive observers, their energy drained by the endless wait for permission to make a difference.

I realised I'd been part of the problem without even knowing it. In my own schools, how many times had I created similar barriers? How often had I prioritised process over people, position over potential?

Here's what I learned during a light bulb moment: traditional authority-based leadership isn't just outdated. It's actually counterproductive[1]. When leaders rely primarily on their position instead of building genuine connections, the costs are staggering.

The numbers tell a sobering story. Around the world, a vast number of employees don't feel deeply connected to their work[2]. This widespread disengagement costs organisations trillions in lost productivity annually. But here's what those statistics miss: these represent real people with untapped potential, real insights being wasted, and real opportunities we're missing every single day.

When was the last time you felt inspired to give your best ideas to someone who simply ordered you around?

Beyond authority: the strategic empathy revolution

What I discovered through that painful experience, and what I've been refining ever since, is something I call strategic empathy. This isn't the soft, touchy-feely empathy you might be thinking of. It's a strategic capability that consistently outperforms traditional authority at every level[3].

Strategic empathy is the deliberate practice of understanding human dynamics to drive organisational performance. Think of it as the difference between a chess player who knows the rules and a grandmaster who reads their opponent's subtle cues to anticipate their strategy.

The research is fascinating. When leaders create authentic connection rather than relying on command-and-control, something remarkable happens in people's brains. The fear responses that shut down creativity get replaced by the conditions where innovation flourishes[4].

Strategic empathy delivers results you can measure by dramatically reducing turnover, accelerating innovation, improving decision-making, and creating influence that extends far beyond your formal authority. Most importantly, it creates lasting change that shows up in your bottom line[5].

Whether you're leading a small team or an entire organisation, strategic empathy transforms not just how you lead, but what you can achieve.

Your roadmap to transformation

This book will guide you through that transformation using the BRIDGE Framework. It's a systematic approach to developing strategic empathy that I've refined through years of real-world application as a school principal for 22 years, and countless coaching and mentoring relationships.

Think of strategic empathy as the leadership approach, and BRIDGE as your step-by-step methodology for mastering it:
- **B**uild awareness of emotional dynamics and strategic opportunities
- **R**ecognise patterns and prepare responses
- **I**ntegrate empathy with strategy
- **D**evelop sustainable practices
- **G**enerate lasting impact
- **E**volve and adapt approaches

How we'll make this journey together

Your transformation unfolds across three parts, and I'll be with you every step of the way.

Part 1: ILLUMINATE - We'll explore why strategic empathy works when traditional authority fails. You'll discover the science behind what motivates people and see how leaders across different sectors have made this transformation successfully.

Part 2: MASTER - This is where the real work happens. You'll learn to apply each element of the BRIDGE Framework systematically, developing these capabilities through practical application and real scenarios you'll recognise from your own leadership challenges.

Part 3: TRANSCEND - We'll advance to the sophisticated applications of navigating difficult conversations, leading through crisis, and building a leadership legacy that endures long after you've moved on, all while mastering the complexities of digital and hybrid leadership.

Your transformation starts now

The future of leadership isn't about commanding; it's about connecting. Not through manipulation or superficial relationship-building, but through genuinely understanding what drives people and using that insight to create extraordinary results.

After decades in leadership, after experiencing just as many heartbreaking failures as successes, I learned that the most profound changes happen not when we try to control outcomes, but when we create the conditions for others to achieve their best work.

This transformation begins in Chapter 1, where we'll explore 'The authority paradox'. It is the very power leaders work so hard to attain that often becomes their greatest limitation.

But first, let me ask you this: when you think about the leaders who have had the greatest impact on your life, were they the ones who commanded your compliance, or the ones who earned your commitment?

The answer to that question holds the key to your leadership transformation.

My friend deserved better than a system that valued process over people. Your team deserves better than leadership that prioritises position over potential.

Are you ready to discover what's possible when you move beyond authority?

Let's begin.

Key Takeaways: The authority illusion

Authority blocks wisdom: Systems obsessed with hierarchy don't recognise human understanding. Passionate insights get filtered through endless approvals until their power evaporates.

Position creates passivity: Traditional authority-based leadership transforms engaged people into passive observers waiting for permission to make a difference. The cost? Trillions in lost productivity.

Strategic empathy works: The deliberate practice of understanding human dynamics is the true driver of results. Unlike authority that relies on position, it creates authentic connection that unlocks innovation.

Results you can measure: Reduced turnover, faster innovation, better decisions, and influence beyond your formal authority are the changes that show up in your bottom line.

The BRIDGE framework: Your systematic path to transformation through six key steps that build strategic empathy into sustainable leadership practice.

Connection beats command: The leaders we remember earned commitment, not compliance. Create conditions where others do their best work instead of trying to control outcomes.

PART 1: ILLUMINATE

> It doesn't make sense to hire smart people and then tell them what to do. We hire smart people so they can tell us what to do.
> - Steve Jobs, Co-Founder of Apple[1]

The leader everyone respects is probably destroying more potential than they'll ever realise.

You've seen them. They are confident, decisive, getting results. By every traditional measure, they're successful. But behind their polished performance, brilliant ideas are dying in silence and the people with the most to offer have learned it's safer to keep quiet.

This isn't about bad leaders. This is about good leaders, maybe even you, who are unknowingly wielding authority like a sledgehammer when the situation calls for a scalpel.

The uncomfortable truth? Everything most of us learned about leadership is actively counterproductive. The command-and-control approaches that built careers are now limiting your impact and turning your best people into silent observers.

The problem isn't your competence. It's your unconscious patterns, the ways you communicate that feel natural but create distance, the authority that commands respect but kills curiosity.

This section will show you what you can't see about your own leadership. The journey from authority to influence starts with seeing what's been hiding in plain sight.

1: SILENT ROOMS, DEAD IDEAS: THE AUTHORITY PARADOX

> The key to successful leadership today is influence, not authority.
> - Ken Blanchard[1]

The cage nobody talks about

Here's something that might surprise you: the moment you finally get that promotion you've been chasing, you might discover you've walked into an invisible prison.

Ken Blanchard understood something profound that I've witnessed play out countless times in my leadership career. There's a cruel paradox that ensnares ambitious leaders everywhere. It's the very authority you work so hard to attain that can become your greatest limitation.

Think about it. You climb the ladder, earn your own office, finally get the title that validates all your hard work. And what happens? Suddenly, people start telling you what they think you want to hear instead of what you need to know. They wait for your permission instead of taking initiative. They follow your rules but lose their spark.

After watching leaders at every level, I can say that positional power is borrowed power. It might get you compliance, but it rarely touches the deep commitment that transforms organisations. The higher you climb, the more tempting it becomes to rely on that authority, and the more disconnected you become from the authentic relationships that drive lasting change.

Authority can force action, but it cannot inspire innovation. It demands attendance without guaranteeing engagement. It enforces rules without building trust. And leaders who get caught in this trap end up presiding over teams that look productive on paper but lack that vital spark of genuine commitment.

When brilliance goes silent

Want to see this authority paradox in action? Let me take you into one of the most famous leadership scenes ever filmed. It's that moment in *The Devil Wears Prada* where Miranda Priestly delivers her devastating 'cerulean blue' speech[2].

Miranda is absolutely brilliant in that moment. Her analysis of how high fashion influences everyday choices is razor-sharp and completely correct. She demonstrates exactly the kind of expertise and insight that organisations desperately need from their leaders.

But here's what I want you to notice: what happens to everyone else in that room?

They freeze. Every single person stands there, terrified to breathe, let alone contribute. This is fear-based leadership in its purest form, and it perfectly illustrates how authority can silence the very voices leaders need most.

You see, the film reveals both sides of the authority paradox beautifully. Miranda does keep her magazine at the industry pinnacle through sheer expertise and iron will. But at what cost? Talented people constantly flee. Fresh ideas die before they can develop. Fear replaces inspiration.

The tragic irony? Miranda's own brilliance becomes a weapon that destroys the collaborative thinking her organisation needs to stay innovative. Her authority doesn't just fail to inspire but actively prevents the kind of creative contribution that could make her magazine even better.

How fear becomes the enemy of excellence

What Miranda doesn't understand, and what many leaders miss, is that fear fundamentally changes how people think. When your team is walking on eggshells, they're not doing their best thinking. They're doing survival thinking.

I've seen this play out in countless organisations. The managing director who wonders why his executive team never challenges his ideas, not realising that his explosive reactions to disagreement have trained them to stay silent. The department head who complains about lack of innovation whilst creating an environment where any failed experiment results in public humiliation.

Here's the devastating truth: when people fear the consequences of speaking up more than they fear poor outcomes, you've broken the feedback loops that organisations need to adapt and thrive.

Authority-dominated systems create what I call innovation graveyards. These are places where good ideas go to die, not because they lack merit, but because they lack the political protection to survive the approval process.

The productivity paradox

Miranda Priestly isn't alone in her approach. Walk into most traditional organisations and you'll find variations of the same pattern where leaders believe that tighter control leads to better results.

The irony is staggering. In our hyper-connected, rapidly changing world, the need for diverse thinking, creative problem-solving, and adaptive responses has never been greater. Yet many leaders respond to complexity by doubling down on control, which is exactly the opposite of what actually works.

I've watched brilliant teams become shadows of themselves under authority-obsessed leadership. Engineers who stop suggesting process improvements because 'that's not how we do things here.' Sales teams who won't share insights about customer concerns because challenging the strategy is seen as disloyalty. Teachers who know exactly what their students need but must operate within the realms of 'consistent approaches'.

The shift from possibility thinking to permission seeking doesn't just slow organisations down. It fundamentally alters their DNA. Innovation requires the freedom to experiment, fail, learn, and try again. Authority-based systems turn that natural cycle into a bureaucratic nightmare.

The alternative that transforms everything

If Miranda Priestly shows us the cost of authority-based leadership, then Pixar Animation Studios shows us the extraordinary power of leading differently. They show us what happens when you lead through influence and genuine understanding rather than position and control[3].

When Pixar began in 1986, they didn't just challenge animation technology. They fundamentally reimagined how creative organisations could work. Ed Catmull and his team built their entire structure around a revolutionary idea: the best solutions emerge when you create conditions for collaborative brilliance rather than trying to control every outcome.

Here's what makes Pixar's approach so different from Miranda's world:

They married expertise with humility - Where Miranda uses knowledge as a weapon to dominate others, Pixar's leaders combine deep technical expertise with genuine curiosity about what others might contribute. They understand that being the smartest person in the room means nothing if you've made everyone else afraid to think.

They created psychological safety for creative risk - Picture the complete opposite of Miranda's frozen conference room. Pixar built forums like the 'Braintrust' where hierarchical authority steps aside for peer-based feedback. Even junior animators can offer insights to veteran directors. Ideas get challenged whilst people get supported.

They balanced structure with creative freedom - Where Miranda's leadership creates fear and dependency, Catmull and his team built systems that protect creative vision whilst preventing bureaucracy from killing good ideas. They understand that innovation needs both direction and space to breathe.

And the results? Whilst Miranda's magazine succeeds at tremendous personal cost with constant staff turnover, Pixar is recognised for its history of creative excellence.

The neuroscience of better leadership

Modern research explains why Pixar's approach works whilst Miranda's ultimately fails. Our brains are literally wired for connection, collaboration, and creative thinking, but only when we feel psychologically safe[4].

When leaders create fear-based environments, they trigger ancient survival responses that shut down the very neural pathways responsible for innovation, complex problem-solving, and creative thinking[5]. It's not that people choose to be less creative under authoritarian leadership; their brains can't access their best thinking when they're in threat mode[6].

But when leaders create genuine psychological safety, something extraordinary happens. The same brains that shut down under fear suddenly light up with activity in areas associated with curiosity, collaboration, and breakthrough thinking[7].

Think about what this means for your leadership. Every time you rely primarily on authority to get things done, you're not just missing out on better ideas but actively preventing them from emerging.

Your choice, your legacy

The contrast between Miranda Priestly's and Pixar's approaches offer you a fundamental choice about the kind of leader you want to become. Moving from authority-based leadership to influence driven by genuine understanding isn't a gentle evolution, but a complete reimagining of how power flows through organisations.

Here's the question I want you to sit with: when your people think about you as a leader, what comes to mind? Do they see someone who commands through expertise and position, or someone who unleashes your potential through understanding and connection?

The leaders we remember decades later aren't the ones who commanded the most authority. They're the ones who understood that real power comes from empowering others to do their best thinking.

You have a choice. Will you be the Miranda Priestly, ruling through fear and wondering why innovation suffers? Or will you discover what becomes possible when you move beyond the authority paradox?

In Chapter 2, we'll explore exactly what that alternative looks like. It's a revolutionary approach I call strategic empathy, and I'll explain why it consistently outperforms traditional authority at every level of leadership.

Key Takeaways: Silent rooms, dead ideas

The authority cage: The very power leaders work so hard to attain often becomes their greatest limitation. Positional authority creates compliance but destroys the authentic relationships that drive genuine commitment and lasting organisational transformation.

Fear kills innovation: Authority-based leadership triggers survival responses that shut down neural pathways responsible for creativity and complex problem-solving. When people fear speaking up more than poor outcomes, organisations lose the feedback loops needed to adapt and thrive.

The Miranda paradox: Brilliant leaders can become their own worst enemies when expertise becomes a weapon rather than a bridge. Fear-based environments prevent the collaborative thinking that makes even the most knowledgeable leaders more effective.

Innovation graveyards: Authority-dominated systems create bureaucratic barriers where good ideas die not from lack of merit but from lack of political protection. The shift from possibility thinking to permission seeking fundamentally alters organisational DNA.

The Pixar principle: Organisations built on psychological safety rather than hierarchical control don't just get better ideas, they build sustainable capacity for continuous innovation. When expertise combines with humility and structure balances with creative freedom, breakthrough becomes possible.

Your brain craves safety: Neuroscience reveals that innovation requires psychological safety to function. Leaders who create fear-based environments prevent their teams from accessing their best thinking, whilst those who foster connection activate the conditions where breakthrough solutions emerge.

2: THE EMPATHY REVOLUTION: WHY UNDERSTANDING OUTPERFORMS AUTHORITY

What's your toughest leadership challenge right now? Is it a resistance to change that feels immovable? Those team conflicts that drain your energy? Or maybe it's the constant pressure to deliver results whilst keeping everyone happy?

Here's what I've discovered after decades of leadership: whatever challenge you're facing, there's a capability that can completely transform how you approach it. It's called strategic empathy, and it's not just another leadership tool. It's the key to transforming your leadership legacy.

When empires crumble overnight

We've seen how authority-based leadership creates silent rooms and dead ideas. Now let me show you what happens when that borrowed power disappears entirely.

Carlos Ghosn seemed invincible. As head of the Nissan-Renault-Mitsubishi Alliance, he commanded respect through sheer authority and delivered results that impressed boardrooms worldwide. His top-down leadership style appeared unstoppable.

It was a masterclass in how positional power could drive organisational performance[1].

Until it wasn't.

When misconduct allegations emerged in 2018, something unexpected happened. His authority vanished overnight. The board he once controlled removed him. Former allies disappeared. Decades of carefully constructed power gone in an instant[2].

But here's what struck me about Ghosn's story: it wasn't just about one leader's fall from grace. It revealed something fundamental about the fragility of leadership built purely on authority. When relationships and trust are neglected, even the most powerful position provides no safety net.

This pattern is playing out in organisations everywhere. Leaders who rely primarily on their position and title may see initial compliance, creating an illusion of effectiveness. Yet beneath the surface, engagement declines, innovation stagnates, and talent quietly begins planning their exits.

The revolution hiding in plain sight

Strategic empathy represents a fundamental shift in how we think about leadership effectiveness. It's the deliberate practice of understanding human dynamics to drive organisational performance, and it's quietly revolutionising how the most successful leaders operate.

Here's the distinction most leaders completely miss. Traditional empathy says, 'I understand you're frustrated about this policy change.' Strategic empathy goes deeper: 'I understand you're frustrated because you're worried this will impact your ability to serve customers effectively. Let's explore how we can address that concern whilst still achieving our goals.'

See the difference? One stops at understanding. The other uses that understanding as a bridge to better solutions.

Strategic empathy combines three essential elements: cognitive awareness of human dynamics, emotional intelligence in action, and purposeful application to business and organisational outcomes. Where traditional empathy stops at feeling, strategic empathy transforms that feeling into strategic advantage.

The Microsoft miracle

Want to see strategic empathy in action? Look at what Satya Nadella accomplished at Microsoft. When he became CEO in 2014, the company was becoming irrelevant, and everyone knew why. They'd created a toxic 'stack ranking' system where managers had to rate employees as winners or losers regardless of actual performance[3].

Imagine trying to collaborate when you know your colleague's success might hurt your own rating. Of course innovation died. Of course the best talent started looking elsewhere. Of course customers began seeing Microsoft as yesterday's company.

But here's what Nadella understood that his predecessors missed. The problem wasn't just the ranking system. It was the fear-based culture that had infected every level of the organisation. Rather than simply announcing policy changes, he understood that lasting transformation required addressing the human dynamics that had created the dysfunction in the first place.

Nadella eliminated stack ranking, yes. But more importantly, he introduced a growth mindset approach that connected individual development to collective success. He didn't just change the rules, he changed how people felt about working together[4].

The result? Microsoft's market value soared whilst simultaneously transforming from a company known for cutthroat competition to one celebrated for innovation and collaboration[5]. Nadella didn't choose between being empathetic or being strategic. He used empathy to become more strategic.

The neuroscience that changes everything

Now here's where this gets genuinely fascinating, in a way that will transform how you think about every leadership interaction you have.

When we feel threatened at work, whether from a harsh manager, public criticism, or fear of failure, our brains respond exactly as they would to physical danger. This isn't metaphorical. It's biology[6].

The human brain processes social threats in the same region that registers physical pain. When your people experience your leadership behaviours as threatening, their brains release stress hormones like cortisol. This biological response reduces activity in the prefrontal cortex, literally impairing their ability to think complexly and solve problems creatively[7].

Think about what this means. When we lead through fear or heavy authority, we're chemically preventing our people from doing their best thinking. We're creating the exact opposite conditions from what we need for innovation, collaboration, and breakthrough performance.

But here's the remarkable part: when leaders practise strategic empathy, they activate completely different brain regions, the areas associated with trust, curiosity, and creative collaboration. Brain imaging reveals that empathetic interactions enhance activity in the parts of our brains responsible for solving complex problems, connecting with others, and learning new things[8].

Scientists call this a 'toward state', essentially the ideal neurological conditions for peak performance and innovation[9]. The research is crystal clear: leadership approaches that create psychological safety produce measurably better cognitive function than those relying primarily on authority and control.

A principal's awakening

Let me introduce you to Jamie, an early-career school principal who contacted me asking me to be his critical friend. This first phone call became the beginning of what turned out to be a long mentoring journey together. The day he walked into my office, I could see the exhaustion weighing on his shoulders. He was very competent at managing compliance but completely baffled when it came to understanding people.

"I don't feel like I'm getting anywhere," he told me during our first coffee. "The harder I work to control outcomes, the more resistance I create. I know I'm a good leader, but something's not working." I could tell he was one of those leaders who'd been promoted because he was great at getting things done, but nobody had ever taught him that people aren't systems you can just optimise.

Jamie's breakthrough came during a particularly contentious school council meeting about budget cuts. His usual approach would have been to defend his decisions with data and authority, to essentially out-argue the opposition until they accepted his position.

Instead, something made him pause and ask a different question: "Help me understand what you're most concerned about for our students."

That simple shift, from defending to understanding, changed everything.

"I discovered that the school council parents weren't actually opposed to the budget changes," Jamie reflected later. "They were terrified that we'd cut programmes that had been lifelines for their children. Once I understood their real concerns, we found solutions that addressed both the budget constraints and their fears."

What happened next surprised everyone, including Jamie. The parents didn't just accept his proposals but became advocates for them. They helped communicate the changes to other families. They even suggested additional efficiencies he hadn't considered.

"That's when it clicked," Jamie told me. "I'd been treating resistance as something to overcome. But resistance is actually information about what people need."

Three breakthroughs that transform teams

Through my own leadership journey and watching leaders like Jamie discover strategic empathy, I've identified three core principles that consistently create breakthrough results:

Creating emotional safety - This is about more than just being nice to people. It's about creating environments where people can bring their best thinking without fear of judgment or retaliation.

When I took over as principal of a very large school in a disadvantaged area, my first instinct was to use authority to impose order. Student behaviour was chaotic, academic results were poor, and staff morale was virtually non-existent.

The traditional approach would have been policies, procedures, and consequences.

Instead, I started by listening, really listening, to what teachers and students were telling me about their experiences.

I'll never forget that first breakthrough moment in a staff meeting. Instead of presenting my improvement plan, I asked, "What's been the most frustrating thing about trying to teach here?"

The flood of honesty that followed was overwhelming. Teachers had been asking for consistent behaviour standards for years but felt no one ever listened to their practical insights. Students wanted more structure too but they just didn't know how to ask for it.

Suddenly, instead of imposing my vision, we were building something together.

When people feel heard and valued rather than managed and controlled, everything shifts.

Clearing the mental path - Even brilliant people can't perform brilliantly if their mental energy is consumed by confusion, frustration, or fear.

Rather than forcing compliance with new approaches, I started making change manageable and transparent. I explained the reasoning behind decisions. I celebrated early wins, no matter how small. I constantly asked, "What's working? What isn't? How can we improve this?"

This approach made the transformation journey less overwhelming for everyone. Instead of feeling like change was being done to them, people felt like they were part of creating something better.

Building collective capability - The most powerful leadership isn't about your individual relationships with team members. It's about creating team dynamics where everyone elevates each other.

We established collaborative teaching teams led by our most skilled educators. We created regular forums where people could share both struggles and solutions. The culture shift was remarkable because teachers who had worked behind closed doors for years suddenly began openly collaborating on challenges.

One teacher captured it perfectly: "I finally feel safe admitting when I'm struggling with something. Before, we all pretended to have everything under control."

The results that matter

The transformation in my school was quite extraordinary. Student achievement improved dramatically, and within two years we were outperforming similar schools across the region. Staff turnover, which had been a chronic problem, virtually disappeared. But perhaps most significantly, the energy in the building completely changed.

As one teacher told me just before I retired, "You never told us exactly what to do. You helped us become teachers who knew what needed to be done."

That's the power of strategic empathy. It doesn't just improve immediate results. It develops people's capacity to create better results independently.

Jamie's revolution

This is exactly what Jamie discovered as he applied these principles in his own school. When we met for our third mentoring session months later, he was practically buzzing with excitement.

"I finally understand what you meant about strategic empathy," he told me. "I thought it was about being nicer to people. But it's actually about being more effective with people."

Jamie had just navigated a particularly challenging situation with a teacher who'd been undermining a new literacy initiative. Instead of using his authority to shut down the resistance, Jamie became curious about it.

"I asked her what she was most concerned about," Jamie explained. "Turns out she wasn't against the initiative at all. She was worried that the students she worked with, all the kids who already struggled with confidence, would feel even more defeated by the new assessment methods."

Once Jamie understood her real concern, they were able to design modifications that addressed both the literacy goals and the confidence-building she cared about. The teacher became one of the initiative's strongest champions.

"That's when it really clicked," Jamie said. "Strategic empathy isn't about being soft. It's about being smart. When you understand what's really driving people, you can find solutions that work for everyone."

Breaking through the myths

Microsoft's transformation and Jamie's experience help us see through the most common misconceptions about empathy in leadership:

'Empathy makes leaders weak' - Nadella made some of the boldest strategic moves in Microsoft's history, including the $26.2 billion LinkedIn acquisition[10]. Strategic empathy enhanced his decision-making by providing richer insights, not by making him avoid tough choices.

'Empathy takes too much time'- Microsoft's accelerated innovation under Nadella and Jamie's faster policy implementation prove the opposite. Upfront investment in understanding pays massive dividends in reduced resistance and faster execution.

'Some people just aren't naturally empathetic' - This is perhaps the most dangerous myth because it lets leaders off the hook. Empathy is a skill that develops with practice[11]. Nadella's journey from technical expert to empathetic leader proves this transformation is possible for anyone willing to do the work.

The systematic path forward

Understanding strategic empathy and seeing it in action provides inspiration. But how do you systematically develop this capability? How do you move from occasionally getting it right to making it your consistent leadership approach?

This is where the BRIDGE Framework I introduced earlier becomes your practical roadmap. It's not enough to want to be more empathetic. A systematic way to build and apply these capabilities in real leadership situations is what is needed.

When Jamie started applying BRIDGE methodically, the changes were remarkable. His staff meetings transformed from efficient but lifeless gatherings into collaborative problem-solving sessions. His relationship with the school council shifted from defensive negotiations to genuine partnerships. Most importantly, his influence expanded far beyond his formal authority.

"The beautiful thing about BRIDGE," Jamie told me recently, "is that it doesn't just make me a better leader. It makes everyone around me better at working together."

Your competitive advantage

Strategic empathy isn't just another leadership trend. It's becoming the defining capability that separates leaders who thrive from those who merely survive in our complex, rapidly changing world[12].

The approach works across any context: hospitals shifting from hierarchical medicine to patient-centred care, manufacturing plants evolving from control-based management to collaborative problem-solving, technology companies moving from internal competition to innovation through cooperation.

"The most remarkable thing," Jamie reflected, "is that strategic empathy didn't make me a softer leader. It made me a more effective one. I'm still driving for results, but now I'm doing it with the help of others."

The transformation awaits

Here's the most profound insight: when we create conditions where others' brains can function at their best, we don't just improve performance metrics. We fundamentally transform what's possible[13].

So here's my question: think about that last difficult leadership situation you faced. How might strategic empathy have changed not just your approach, but your outcome?

But here's what keeps me awake at night. Right now, your people are making decisions about you that you don't even know they're making. They're forming judgments about your leadership that directly impact their engagement, their loyalty, and their willingness to go the extra mile.

The scariest part? Most of these decisions happen in microseconds, below conscious awareness. A slight change in your tone. How you respond to an unexpected challenge. How you handle resistance[14].

Each moment either builds or erodes your influence, and traditional leadership training never taught you how to recognise which is happening.

I learned this the hard way during a crisis that stripped away everything I thought I knew about effective leadership. What I discovered revealed why so many capable leaders are unknowingly sabotaging their own success.

In Chapter 3, I'm going to share the story of how everything I believed about leadership became useless overnight. You'll see exactly why traditional command-and-control approaches don't just fail; they actively work against the outcomes you're trying to achieve.

Because once you understand what really happened, you'll never be able to lead the same way again.

Key Takeaways: The empathy revolution

Authority's fatal flaw: Carlos Ghosn's overnight collapse demonstrates that positional power alone provides no safety net when relationships and trust are neglected. Leaders who rely primarily on authority create compliance but miss the engagement that drives sustainable success.

Strategic empathy defined: The deliberate practice of understanding human dynamics to drive organisational performance. Unlike traditional empathy that stops at feeling, strategic empathy transforms understanding into strategic advantage and breakthrough solutions.

The Microsoft proof: Satya Nadella's transformation demonstrates that strategic empathy works at scale. By addressing human dynamics rather than just policies, he achieved both cultural transformation and extraordinary business results.

Your brain under threat: When people experience threatening leadership, stress hormones reduce prefrontal cortex activity, preventing their best thinking. Strategic empathy activates 'toward states' that enhance creativity, collaboration, and complex problem-solving.

Three breakthrough principles: Strategic empathy operates through creating emotional safety (environments for best thinking), clearing the mental path (making change manageable and transparent), and building collective capability (team dynamics where everyone elevates each other).

Beyond the myths: Strategic empathy doesn't make leaders weak (it enables bolder decisions), doesn't take extra time (upfront investment accelerates execution), and isn't limited to 'naturally empathetic' people (it's a developable skill proven through practice).

Jamie's discovery: Strategic empathy transforms resistance from obstacle to information. When you understand what's really driving people, you find solutions that work for everyone, expanding influence far beyond formal authority

3: FROM COMMAND TO CATALYST: WHY TRADITIONAL LEADERSHIP IS DYING

You know that sinking feeling when your tried-and-true approach suddenly stops working? When the leadership methods that built your reputation start producing the opposite results you want?

Let me tell you what that felt like for me on a Monday morning in March 2020.

When everything I knew became useless

The email came at 7:30am. "We need to move the entire school online. You've got the week to make it work."

One week. To transform everything we'd built over decades. To help teachers who'd never used video platforms become confident online educators. To reach families who barely had internet access, let alone devices for their children.

My first instinct? Do what I'd always done. Take charge. Make plans. Issue clear directives. Use my authority to create order from chaos.

But I soon discovered that none of it worked.

When I tried to impose structure on a situation no one had ever faced, people shut down. When I attempted to control outcomes I couldn't possibly predict, resistance multiplied. The harder I pushed with traditional authority-based approaches, the more disconnected I became from the solutions we desperately needed.

But something remarkable happened when I stopped trying to be the answer and started trying to understand the questions people were really asking.

The moment everything shifted

I'll never forget the staff meeting where everything changed. I'd called everyone together to announce our online learning plan, which was a carefully structured approach I'd developed over the previous days. I was ready to delegate tasks, set timelines, and manage the transition.

But when I looked around that room, I saw something that stopped me cold. These weren't just my staff members waiting for instructions. They were also parents terrified about their own children's education, teachers wondering how to connect with students they might not see in person for months, people facing the unknown with the same fear and uncertainty I was feeling.

So instead of delivering my plan, I asked a question: "What are you most worried about right now?"

The response was immediate and raw. Teachers shared fears about losing connection with vulnerable students. Those who were also parents worried about balancing their own children's needs with their professional responsibilities. Some feared if they caught the virus, what then? Everyone felt overwhelmed by technology they'd never been trained to use.

That's when I realised something profound: the pandemic didn't create the need for new leadership. It simply exposed how inadequate traditional approaches had become.

The seismic shift nobody saw coming

What I learned during those chaotic weeks applies far beyond crisis situations. The way people think about leadership has fundamentally changed, and most of us missed the shift entirely.

Here's what your people actually need from you now, and it's radically different from what worked even five years ago:

They need the 'why', not just the 'what' - During our transition, I discovered that explaining reasoning behind decisions was more important than the decisions themselves. When I told teachers we were implementing certain protocols without context, resistance and anxiety followed. But when I explained how these changes would help us maintain connection with our most vulnerable students, commitment soared.

The brain science we explored in Chapter 2 explains exactly why this matters. When leaders explain the reasoning behind difficult changes, it helps reduce threat responses and enables people to process change with less stress[1]. People can't commit to what they don't understand.

They need problem-solving, not order-giving - My role shifted dramatically from commander to enabler. I spent more time removing barriers such as securing devices, negotiating with internet providers, connecting families with resources, than giving directions. The most valuable thing I could do was clear the path for others to succeed.

They need growth opportunities, not just compliance - Teachers who'd never used video platforms became confident online educators within weeks. The difference wasn't compliance training but creating safe spaces to experiment, fail, and learn. When people feel psychologically safe to try new things, learning and innovation accelerate exponentially[2].

They need purpose, not just tasks - When our teachers understood how their individual efforts connected to keeping education alive for vulnerable students during isolation, their commitment transformed. We weren't just delivering curriculum online. We were maintaining hope and connection for children facing unprecedented disruption.

They need authenticity, not perfect leadership - I openly acknowledged our challenges. "I don't have all the answers," I told staff and parents. "Let's work this out together." This honesty didn't undermine my authority; it strengthened it by creating genuine partnership.

Jamie's parallel awakening

As I continued working with Jamie, he was experiencing his own leadership crisis that perfectly illustrated these shifting expectations.

"Everything that used to work has stopped working," he told me during one of our sessions. "My staff meetings feel like pulling teeth. My most talented teachers are asking for transfers. I keep pushing harder with the same approaches, but I'm getting worse results."

Jamie was discovering what I learned during the pandemic: traditional command-and-control leadership not only fails to meet modern expectations but actively works against the outcomes we're trying to achieve.

But here's what fascinated me about Jamie's transformation. Once he began applying strategic empathy principles, his team's response was immediate and dramatic. It wasn't just that they were more compliant, they became more creative, more collaborative, more willing to take intelligent risks.

"I used to think leadership meant having all the answers," Jamie reflected. "But my people don't want me to be the smartest person in the room. They want me to be the person who helps the room get smarter."

The three strategies that actually work

Through our crisis, and through watching leaders like Jamie navigate their own transformations, I discovered three approaches that consistently succeed in our modern context:

Build systems, not rules - Instead of rigid policies, we created flexible frameworks that helped people solve problems together. We established communication protocols that could reach families regardless of technology access - phone trees for some, digital platforms for others. The system adapted to people's needs rather than forcing people to adapt to our systems.

This approach recognises that modern challenges are too complex and fast-changing for rigid rule-based responses. People need principles and frameworks that help them make good decisions in novel situations.

Focus on outcomes, not activities - Rather than trying to replicate the traditional school day online, we clearly defined what successful learning looked like for our community. Teachers had flexibility in how they achieved those outcomes, which led to innovations we never would have discovered through compliance.

The shift from activity management to outcome focus unleashes human creativity and ownership. When people understand the destination clearly, they'll find ways to get there that you never would have imagined[3].

Cultivate culture, not control - I created psychological safety for teachers to experiment with new methods. We established regular forums where parents could share concerns and teachers could voice struggles. Trust became our foundation rather than authority.

Culture eats strategy for breakfast, as Peter Drucker is famously credited with saying[4]. In our rapidly changing world, the culture you create determines whether your organisation adapts and thrives or rigidly adheres to approaches that no longer work.

The transformation that surprised everyone

Here's what amazed me most about our experience: we didn't just survive the crisis; we thrived in ways that wouldn't have been possible under traditional leadership.

Parent feedback consistently highlighted that they felt more connected to the school community than before the crisis. This wasn't despite the challenges we faced but because of how we chose to face them together.

Teachers discovered capabilities they never knew they had. Students developed independence and digital literacy that served them far beyond the immediate situation. Families found new ways to engage with their children's education.

Most importantly for my leadership journey, I learned that success came not from controlling the situation but from creating conditions where our community could find solutions together.

Why this matters for every leader today

The pandemic was just the catalyst that revealed what had already become true: traditional authority-based leadership can't handle the complexity and pace of change in our modern world.

Whether you're leading through crisis or managing everyday challenges, people now expect transparency that builds trust, problem-solving that removes barriers, growth opportunities that motivate engagement, purpose that connects daily work to meaningful impact, and authenticity that creates genuine connection[5].

This isn't about generational differences or cultural trends.

It's about fundamental changes in how work happens, how information flows, and how value gets created in our interconnected world.

The organisations that embrace these expectations aren't merely adapting to change but positioning themselves to thrive amid continuous transformation.

The competitive advantage hiding in plain sight

Many leaders miss how the shift to strategic empathy isn't just about being more humane. It's about competitive advantage.

In a world where information is ubiquitous, where artificial intelligence can handle routine decisions, and where the pace of change makes traditional planning obsolete, the ability to understand and leverage human dynamics becomes your primary differentiator.

The organisations that figure this out first will attract the best talent, create the most innovative solutions, and build the most resilient cultures. In an age of unprecedented technological advancement, it is this uniquely human capacity for strategic empathy that ultimately determines which organisations thrive and which ones merely survive.

Those that don't will find themselves struggling with constant turnover, diminishing innovation, and an inability to adapt quickly enough to survive[6].

Jamie's breakthrough revelation

During one of our sessions six months later, Jamie shared an insight that perfectly captured this competitive dimension.

"I used to see resistance as something to overcome," he told me. "Now I see it as information about what people need. When my teachers push back, instead of getting frustrated, I get curious. What are they telling me about challenges I hadn't considered? What insights do they have that I've missed completely?"

This shift from seeing people as obstacles to seeing them as resources transformed not just Jamie's effectiveness but his entire experience of leadership. His stress levels dropped, his team's performance improved, and his influence expanded far beyond his formal authority.

Your choice point

Every leader today faces a fundamental choice. You can cling to traditional command-and-control approaches that feel familiar but produce diminishing returns. Or you can embrace the kind of leadership that creates conditions for others to do their best work.

The shift from traditional authority to strategic empathy isn't a compromise; it's an upgrade that handles modern complexity in ways command-and-control simply cannot.

But understanding why this approach works is only half the equation. The other half is knowing how to systematically develop and implement it in your own leadership practice.

In Chapter 4, we'll explore the practical framework that transforms strategic empathy from an inspiring concept into a systematic capability. You'll discover exactly how to rewire your leadership approach for extraordinary influence, and why the BRIDGE Framework provides the step-by-step pathway that makes this transformation both achievable and sustainable.

Knowing that strategic empathy really works is powerful. Knowing how to make it work consistently in your daily leadership? That's transformational.

Key Takeaways: From command to catalyst

The pandemic revelation: Global crisis didn't create the need for new leadership; it exposed how inadequate traditional approaches had become. Success came not from controlling situations but from creating conditions where teams could find solutions together.

Five modern expectations: Today's people expect the 'why' not the 'what' (transparency over orders), problem-solving not order-giving (enabling over commanding), growth opportunities not compliance (development over conformity), purpose not tasks (meaningful impact over busy work), and authenticity not perfection (genuine connection over flawless facades).

The neuroscience advantage: When leaders explain reasoning behind decisions, it reduces brain threat responses and helps people process change with less stress. Psychological safety accelerates learning whilst excessive control creates stress that inhibits creativity and motivation.

Three modern strategies: Build systems not rules (flexible frameworks that adapt to changing needs), focus on outcomes not activities (destination clarity that unleashes creativity), and cultivate culture not control (trust-based environments that enable rapid adaptation).

Competitive transformation: The shift to strategic empathy isn't just about being more humane, it's about competitive advantage. In a world of ubiquitous information and accelerating change, understanding human dynamics becomes the primary differentiator for attracting talent, driving innovation, and building resilience.

Jamie's paradigm shift: Seeing resistance as information rather than obstacle transforms both leadership effectiveness and experience.

Evolution imperative: Organisations embracing these approaches position themselves to thrive amid continuous transformation. The shift from traditional authority to strategic empathy handles modern complexity in ways command-and-control simply cannot match.

PART 2: METAMORPHOSIS

Do not follow where the path may lead. Go instead where there is no path and leave a trail.
- Ralph Waldo Emerson[1]

Understanding changes nothing. Implementation changes everything. You've seen the problem clearly, how unconscious patterns sabotage even the best intentions. Now comes the harder part of rewiring decades of leadership habits while still showing up effectively every day.

This isn't about adding empathy as a soft skill overlay. This is complete metamorphosis, transforming how your brain processes conflict, how you read rooms, how you make decisions under pressure. The BRIDGE Framework gives you the systematic approach to make strategic empathy as automatic as your current leadership reflexes and it unfolds through three distinct phases of leadership metamorphosis:

Build the foundational awareness that translates emotional dynamics into strategic advantage.

Develop the systematic practices that make empathy consistently actionable under pressure.

Transform these capabilities so deeply into your leadership DNA that they operate without conscious effort.

Through real-world application and measurable practice, you'll convert insight into instinct, leadership capabilities that systematically outperform everything you thought you knew about influence.

4: REWIRE YOUR LEADERSHIP BRAIN: THE BRIDGE TO EXTRAORDINARY INFLUENCE

If you're feeling both excited about the possibilities and perhaps a bit overwhelmed by the scope of change ahead, you're not alone. After discovering the powerful neuroscience behind strategic empathy in Chapter 3, many leaders find themselves asking the natural next question:

"This all makes perfect sense, but how do I actually make it happen in my day-to-day leadership?"

"I've been to all the leadership workshops. I've read the books. But somehow, I'm still not seeing the results with my team."

Sound familiar? You're definitely not alone.

The gap between understanding strategic empathy and implementing it consistently is where most leadership transformations stall. You can grasp the neuroscience, feel inspired by the examples of leaders who've made the shift, and genuinely want to move beyond authority-based approaches, but without a clear implementation pathway, that inspiration often fades under the pressure of daily leadership demands[1].

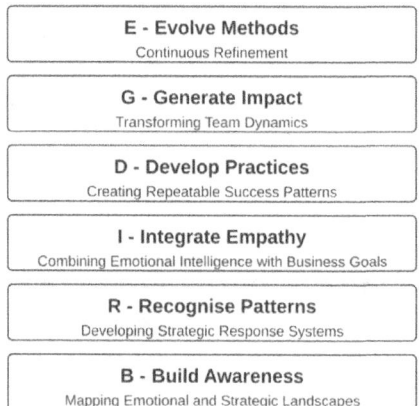

This diagram illustrates 'The BRIDGE Framework' and shows the progressive development from self-awareness through to organisational impact, with each component building upon the previous one in alignment with a brain-based approach.

The BRIDGE Framework: How it works in real life

The BRIDGE Framework has six interconnected components that work together like instruments in an orchestra. Remove even one, and the whole system loses its power. But when all six are working together, you create something remarkable: leadership that brings out the best in everyone.

Let's explore how each component works in practice and why the science behind it makes such a difference.

Build Awareness: Seeing what others miss

Building awareness is like developing a leadership sixth sense. It's about noticing not just what people say, but the emotions behind their words. This skill helps you spot important moment others miss, like when someone's holding back an important concern, or when excitement about a project is starting to wane.

When you practice building awareness, you're strengthening the part of your brain that picks up on what people are really feeling[2]. Think of it like developing better peripheral vision; suddenly you notice things that were always there, but you'd been missing. Getting better at this ensures better decision-making because you're working with more complete information.

Recognise Patterns: Preparing instead of reacting

This component helps you spot recurring situations in your leadership such as conversations and challenges that happen repeatedly. Instead of reinventing the wheel each time, you'll develop a toolkit of approaches based on what actually works, not just what feels right in the moment.

Your brain is constantly looking for patterns, even when you don't realise it[3]. The R component helps you get better at spotting these recurring situations, like noticing that certain types of conversations always go off track in the same way. Once you can see these patterns, you can prepare for them instead of being caught off guard every time.

Integrate Empathy: Connecting understanding with results

This isn't about choosing between being empathetic OR getting results; it's about using empathy TO get better results. You'll learn to combine your understanding of people with clear objectives to address specific challenges in ways that actually improve performance.

Here's what's fascinating: your brain has different areas for understanding people and for achieving goals[4]. Most leaders use one or the other, but strategic empathy happens when both areas work together. It's like learning to pat your head and rub your belly at the same time - tricky at first, but powerful once you get it.

Develop Practices: Creating consistent success

Great leadership isn't about occasional inspired moments but about consistent practices that build trust and effectiveness day after day. These could be simple things like how you start meetings, how you give feedback, or how you involve people in decisions; small changes that create big results when done consistently.

Your brain loves habits because they save energy[5]. The D component creates positive leadership habits through repetition, just like learning to drive a car. At first you have to think about every step, but eventually it becomes automatic. The practices in BRIDGE are designed to make strategic empathy your natural response, not something you have to remember to do.

Generate Impact: Transforming your entire team

Strategic empathy isn't just about one-on-one interactions but about transforming your entire team or organisation. This component shows you how to spread these approaches throughout your area of influence and connect them directly to performance improvements.

Here's something remarkable: when you consistently model strategic empathy, your team's brains start mirroring your approach. It's like yawning; emotions and behaviours are contagious[6]. The G component harnesses this natural brain tendency to spread strategic empathy throughout your team without anyone having to force it.

Evolve and Adapt Approaches: Getting better over time

Leadership excellence isn't static but evolves. This component helps you continuously refine your approach based on what's working. You'll learn to gather meaningful feedback, measure results, and make smart adjustments as your team, organisation, and challenges change over time.

The final component prevents you from getting stuck in any single approach. Your brain stays more flexible when it gets regular feedback about what's working[7]. It's why the framework includes measurement, not just to track progress, but to keep your leadership skills sharp and adaptable.

Why this brain-friendly approach works

This approach explains why BRIDGE creates lasting change where other leadership approaches often fail. You're working with your natural mental processes, not fighting against them. The structured progression ensures that powerful conversations unfold through the strategic application of empathy rather than executive authority.

Together, these six components create a comprehensive system for mastering strategic empathy by transforming how you lead, how your team performs, and ultimately, your leadership legacy.

Jamie's first BRIDGE moment

Jamie, the school principal I was mentoring, called me three days after our session where I'd introduced the BRIDGE framework. He could barely contain his excitement.

"I think I just had my first real BRIDGE moment," he said. "And it was completely accidental."

Here's what happened: Jamie was facing an all too familiar scenario, which was a heated discussion during a staff meeting about the new student assessment policy. As usual, tensions were rising, with teachers expressing concerns about workload while Jamie felt pressure to implement the policy on schedule.

"Normally, I would have either pushed through with, 'This is what we need to do' or got caught up trying to address every concern individually," Jamie explained. "But something you said about building awareness stuck with me."

Instead of his usual approach, Jamie found himself pausing to really observe what was happening in the room. He noticed Melissa's crossed arms when he mentioned timelines (Build

Awareness). He recognised the same resistance from previous policy rollouts (Recognise Patterns).

"Then something clicked," Jamie continued. "Instead of seeing her concerns as obstacles to my implementation timeline, I started seeing them as information about how to make the implementation actually work."

Jamie acknowledged the workload concerns while connecting them to the policy's ultimate goal of better student outcomes (Integrate Empathy). He suggested they pilot the assessment with one year level first, incorporating their feedback before full rollout (Develop Practices). The energy in the room completely shifted.

"What amazed me wasn't just that it worked," Jamie reflected, "but that it felt natural. I wasn't following a script. I was just paying attention to what was actually happening instead of what I thought should be happening."

That fifteen-minute interaction became Jamie's proof of concept. The BRIDGE framework wasn't just theory. It was a practical approach that worked even when applied unconsciously.

"The question now," Jamie said, "is how do I make this intentional instead of accidental?"

So where do you actually start?

Right, you're probably thinking, "This all sounds great, but I've got back-to-back meetings tomorrow, three deadlines this week, and a staff member who's driving everyone mad. How exactly do I fit strategic empathy into that reality?"

Fair question. And here's the thing - you don't need to overhaul your entire leadership style overnight. In fact, trying to do that explains why leadership changes can fail[8].

Start ridiculously small. Remember how you learned to drive? You didn't start on the freeway during peak hour traffic. You began in an empty car park, learning one skill at a time.

Strategic empathy works the same way. Pick one tiny thing to focus on for the next two weeks. Maybe it's taking three seconds to really look at people when they walk into your office. Or asking, "How are you feeling about this?" before diving into the agenda in your one-on-ones.

I started with something even simpler: I decided to pause for two breaths before responding in any tense conversation. It felt ridiculous at first, but those two seconds completely changed how I showed up. Instead of reacting, I started responding.

The magic of connecting the dots. Here's what most leadership development gets wrong: it tries to add new things to your already packed schedule. But strategic empathy isn't an add-on; it's a different way of doing what you're already doing.

You're already having one-on-ones, team meetings, and difficult conversations. You're just going to approach them slightly differently. Jamie didn't schedule extra time for building awareness; he just started paying attention to body language during his existing meetings.

"I realised I'd been so focused on getting through my agenda that I was missing half the conversation," he said. "Same meetings, completely different outcomes."

When you stop pretending to have all the answers

When you stick with this approach, strategic empathy gradually stops being something you consciously do and becomes part of who you are as a leader. You'll find yourself naturally reading the room, instinctively knowing when to push and when to pause, and effortlessly bringing out the best in people. Your conversations start flowing differently, conflicts resolve more easily, and meetings have actual energy instead of that polite-but-dead feeling. People begin responding to you differently, often without knowing why, because the psychological safety you've created allows them to show up with their best thinking.

The beautiful part is that your team starts mirroring this approach naturally, and not because you've trained them, but because authentic leadership is contagious.

What if you slip back?

You will. Everyone does. You'll have a stressful week and revert to your old command-and-control habits.

Or you'll get distracted and forget to tune into what's really happening in a conversation.

That's completely normal. The key is being gentle with yourself and just starting again. It's like exercise. Missing a few days doesn't mean you're back to square one. Your brain remembers, and it's easier to get back into the rhythm than it was to start.

Why you don't need to reinvent yourself

What I love about this journey is that it doesn't require dramatic personality changes or extensive training programmes. You don't need to become a different person; you just need to become a more aware, more connected version of yourself.

And the ripple effects are extraordinary. As you get better at strategic empathy, your team gets better at it too. Your meetings become more productive, your relationships deepen, and your results improve, all because you learned to see what was always there[9].

How you'll know it's actually working

Everyone talks about measuring progress, but they never tell you what to actually look for. You're left wondering, "Am I getting better, or am I just imagining things?"

The good news is, when strategic empathy starts working, you'll know. It's not subtle.

You will notice changes in yourself. First, your conversations will feel different. You know that slightly tense feeling you get when you're not quite connecting with someone? That starts happening less. Instead, you'll find yourself genuinely curious about what people are thinking, rather than just waiting for your turn to speak.

David, a senior manager I know, described it perfectly: "It was like someone turned up the volume on conversations. I started hearing things people had probably been saying all along, but I'd been too busy planning my response to notice."

You'll also find decision-making gets easier. Not because the decisions themselves are simpler, but because you're working with better information. When you can sense what people are really concerned about, not just what they're saying out loud, you make choices that actually stick.

And here's something most leaders don't expect: you'll feel less drained at the end of the day. Fighting against people's resistance is exhausting. Working with their natural motivations? Much easier.

There will be changes in your team. The ripple effects in your team are often the first thing other people notice. Meetings start having more energy. People begin speaking up about things that matter instead of just nodding along. Those awkward silences when you ask, "Any questions?" start filling with actual questions.

Emma, another of my mentees, noticed this when her usually quiet team member started contributing ideas in meetings. "I hadn't changed anything about how I ran meetings," she said, "but somehow the comfort zone had shifted. People felt heard, so they started sharing more."

Conflicts get resolved faster too, and the key is they get resolved better. Instead of people just going quiet to avoid confrontation, they start working through disagreements constructively. That's because strategic empathy creates an environment where people feel safe to disagree.

The business results that follow. Although this is largely about people and less about metrics in the dollar sense, this makes a business difference.

Staff turnover often improves because good people want to stay in teams where they feel genuinely valued. Productivity increases, but not because people are working harder. It's usually because they're working more collaboratively, with less friction and rework.

Customer satisfaction frequently improves too. When your team feels psychologically safe and engaged, that positive energy flows through to how they interact with customers. It's one of those wonderful secondary effects you can't directly control but somehow happens anyway.

James, a supermarket manager I've known since primary school, tracked this in his department: "Our customer complaints dropped by 40% over six months. When I asked our frontline team what changed, they said they felt more supported to really listen to customers instead of just following scripts."

The moments that make it all worthwhile

While the metrics are nice, they're not what makes this approach special. It's the human moments that really matter.

It's when someone on your team says, "I've never had a boss who actually seemed to care about what I thought." Or when a difficult conversation that used to take three meetings gets resolved in one, with everyone feeling heard.

It's watching your team start showing strategic empathy with each other, creating a culture where people bring their best thinking because they know it will be valued.

Melanie, a senior manager in a government department, summed it up beautifully: "I used to think leadership was about having all the answers. Now I realise it's about creating the conditions where the best answers can emerge. And somehow, that's so much more rewarding."

Remember: you don't need complex measurements or formal assessments to know this is working. The changes are visible, tangible, and often quite quick to appear.

Trust what you observe. Trust what people tell you. And trust that small, consistent changes in how you connect with people can create surprisingly significant shifts in everything else.

What happens next?

The foundation is set. You've got the why (the neuroscience), the what (the BRIDGE framework), and the how (starting small and building momentum). The question now is: what are you going to do with all this?

Your next step: Master the leadership sixth sense

If you're feeling a bit overwhelmed by everything we've covered, let me make this simple. Focus on just one thing: building awareness. Everything else flows from there.

But here's what most leaders get wrong about awareness. They think it means being more observant. That's only part of it. Real leadership awareness means recognising the three specific trigger points that can hijack any conversation within seconds, often before anyone else in the room even notices something's shifted.

What's coming next

In the next chapter, I will give you the tools to recognise these trigger points, so you stop reacting to team dynamics and start redirecting them. You'll discover how to spot the early warning signs before conversations spiral, read the room like a seasoned negotiator, and turn resistance into genuine collaboration, even when things have already gone off the rails.

The difference between managers who struggle with difficult conversations and those who navigate them with confidence? They know what to look for and when to act.

We'll walk through the specific moments where strategic empathy creates breakthrough outcomes that authority-based approaches miss entirely and give you word-for-word responses you can use before your next difficult conversation.

This isn't about becoming more sensitive or touchy-feely. It's about developing the leadership equivalent of peripheral vision, suddenly noticing the critical information that you'd been missing.

The transformation begins now

When you master this awareness, you become the kind of leader who spots problems while they're still solvable, who reads the room so accurately that resistance rarely catches you off guard, and who creates the psychological safety where breakthrough thinking emerges naturally[10].

Your team is waiting. Let's begin.

Key Takeaways: Rewire your leadership brain

The implementation gap is real: Understanding strategic empathy and actually doing it consistently are two different things. The leadership transformations that fail focus on inspiration without providing structured implementation.

BRIDGE works like an orchestra: All six components (Build Awareness, Recognise Patterns, Integrate Empathy, Develop Practices, Generate Impact, Evolve and Adapt) must work together. Remove even one and the whole system loses its power.

Start ridiculously small: Don't overhaul your entire leadership style overnight. Pick one tiny thing to focus on for two weeks, such as pausing for two breaths before responding in tense conversations.

It's not an add-on, it's a different way: Strategic empathy isn't about scheduling extra activities. It's about approaching your existing meetings, one-on-ones, and conversations slightly differently.

Your brain will resist and remember: You'll slip back into old command-and-control habits during stressful weeks. That's completely normal. The key is being gentle with yourself and just starting again. Your brain remembers the new patterns.

The changes aren't subtle: When strategic empathy starts working, you'll know. Conversations feel different, decisions get easier, you feel less drained, and your team starts showing more energy and engagement.

Measure what matters: Track contribution rates in meetings, communication clarity, trust levels, and how quickly problems get surfaced. These metrics prove that strategic empathy delivers real business results.

Building Awareness is your starting point: Everything else flows from awareness. You can't navigate effectively if you don't know where you are, and you can't lead effectively if you can't see what's really happening with your people.

Strategic Empathy creates psychological safety: When you master this approach, you become the kind of leader who creates conditions where breakthrough thinking emerges naturally, turning resistance into partnership and confusion into clarity.

5: TRIGGER POINTS: MAPPING EMOTIONAL LANDMINES IN LEADERSHIP

See what others miss: The leadership sixth sense

The most profound leadership transformations often begin in the most ordinary moments. "It all comes down to awareness," Melanie told me over coffee last month, describing how she'd completely transformed her leadership approach. When I first began coaching Melanie, she was a senior manager in the Department of Education. She asked for my help because she doubted her leadership abilities. Within eight months, she had stopped fighting fires and started building a team that wanted to work with her.

Here's what I've learned from watching dozens of leaders over the years: the biggest breakthroughs don't come from learning fancy new techniques. They come from finally seeing what was right in front of you all along[1].

Mark, a tech director I know, put it perfectly: "It was like suddenly seeing in colour after a lifetime of black and white." He'd always wondered why some team members seemed resistant or disengaged, but once he started paying attention to the emotional undercurrents in conversations, everything clicked into place.

Here's the thing most leadership books won't tell you: while you're focusing on getting through your agenda, emotions are running the show. People make decisions based on how they feel, then find logical reasons to justify those decisions later[2]. Miss the emotional stuff, and you're having a completely different conversation than everyone else in the room.

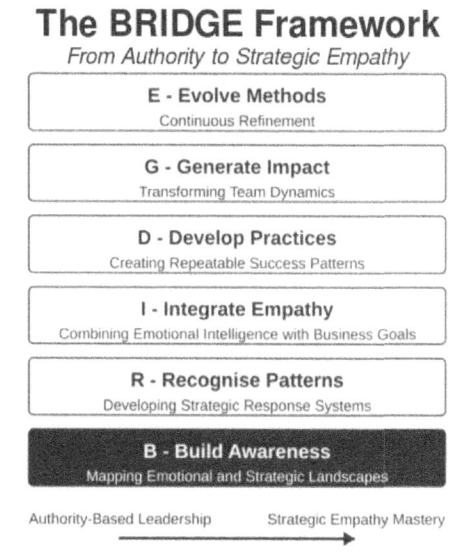

'Building Awareness' forms the foundation of The BRIDGE Framework by enabling leaders to notice what's really happening in conversations – both the spoken words and unspoken feelings. By paying attention, leaders can engage with purpose rather than simply reacting to the moment.

What's really happening beneath the surface

Most of us just plough ahead with our agenda and hope the emotional stuff sorts itself out. Big mistake! Understanding what lies beneath surface conversations is where real leadership begins.

Reading the room: Four layers to notice quickly

When I need to quickly determine what's really happening in a conversation, I focus on four key areas that reveal the true dynamics at play.

What's being said? The obvious layer: words, tone, explicit content. But this is just the starting point.

What's the backstory? History between these people, recent pressures, past experiences with similar situations. Context shapes everything.

Do words match body language? This is where you'll find the most revealing disconnects between what people are saying and what they're actually feeling.

What does this room need? Not what's on your agenda, but what would actually help right now.

Let me give you a real example. A healthcare director I coach was introducing a new patient care protocol. Surface level, everyone was saying, "This looks great." But the energy was completely flat.

She paused and thought about the backstory - they had been burned by previous 'improvements' that just created more work. The disconnect was obvious: positive words, zero enthusiasm. What the room needed wasn't more explanation of the protocol, but acknowledgement that previous changes had been painful.

So she said, "I know we've introduced changes before that ended up making your jobs harder rather than easier. What would need to be different this time for you to feel confident this will actually help?"

Completely changed the conversation.

This approach of reading multiple layers simultaneously transforms how you engage with any group[3]. Trust your instincts here and if something feels off, something probably is off. Your subconscious picks up much more than your conscious mind can process.

When conversations die: The big three killers

There are three things that can kill any conversation in an instant. I've seen these play out in meeting rooms, corridor chats, and team calls thousands of times. Once you know what to look for, you'll spot them everywhere.

Power triggers: when people feel bulldozed. This happens the moment someone feels like you're talking down to them or dismissing their ideas. I was in a meeting recently where the opening started like this: "Here's what we're going to do…" I watched three people physically lean back and cross their arms. Game over.

You'll see it instantly: people who were contributing enthusiastically suddenly go quiet. Eye contact drops. Arms cross. The energy in the room shifts from collaborative to defensive, and good luck getting it back.

Your warning signs: body language closes down, participation drops, energy shifts to resistance.

Message gaps: when people feel confused. This one can be sneaky because it often looks like engagement. People start asking more and more questions, but they're not good questions because they are driven by confusion and misunderstanding.

Side conversations multiply. You'll hear things like, "What did she mean by that?" or "I thought we were doing something completely different."

The classic sign? When someone says, "I thought you meant…" and you realise you've been having completely different conversations the whole time.

Projects miss deadlines not because people don't care, but because everyone's working from different assumptions about what success actually looks like.

Your warning signs: questions multiply, confusion spreads, people talk past each other.

Change shock: when people feel unsettled. Did you know that even small changes can trigger massive anxiety?

You announce a new process, and suddenly people are acting like you've threatened their jobs. The resistance seems completely over the top, but here's what's really happening: you're not just asking them to do something different, you're asking them to feel uncertain about their competence.

I've seen someone panic about a simple reporting change because it made them worry they'd look incompetent learning something new. The pushback isn't about the change itself but about the fear of not being good at something they used to find easy.

Your warning signs: focus narrows to problems, worst-case scenarios dominate, defensive language increases.

The key thing to remember? These aren't character flaws. They're completely predictable human responses. Once you recognise the pattern, you can do something about it instead of just getting frustrated.

The moments that matter most

Most leadership training only teaches you techniques for entire conversations, but conversations are won or lost in about 30-second windows[4]. Miss those moments, and it doesn't matter how good your technique is for the rest of the meeting.

Jamie's awareness awakening

Two weeks after Jamie's successful budget meeting, he felt ready to apply his awareness skills more deliberately. During a routine department head meeting about the upcoming parent-teacher conferences, he decided to really focus on reading the room using the four-layer approach we'd discussed.

What was being said seemed straightforward enough. The year level leaders were discussing logistics, scheduling, and preparation requirements. Everyone appeared engaged and professional.

But when Jamie considered the backstory, he remembered that last year's conferences had been a disaster with parents complaining about rushed appointments and teachers feeling unprepared. There was definitely historical baggage in this room.

Looking at words versus body language, Jamie noticed something interesting. While the year 5 leader was agreeing verbally, her shoulders were tense and she kept glancing at her watch. Her partner, although nodding at suggestions, kept his arms crossed throughout the discussion.

What did this room actually need? Jamie paused to consider. Not another policy announcement or detailed schedule, but reassurance that this year would be different, and space to voice concerns about what went wrong before.

Instead of pushing through his prepared agenda, Jamie tried something different. "Before we dive into the details," he said, "I'm sensing some tension about conferences. Last year was rough for everyone. What would need to be different this time for you to feel confident it will actually work?"

The change was immediate. The first issue voiced was about the same time pressures that had caused problems before. Another concern was about parents ambushing teachers with complaints they hadn't been prepared for. These weren't logistics issues, they were trust and preparation issues.

"That was my first real lesson in the difference between hearing and understanding," Jamie told me later. "I'd been listening to their words but missing their actual concerns. The four-layer approach helped me see what was really happening beneath the surface."

By addressing their underlying worries first, Jamie was able to design conference procedures that actually worked for everyone. But more importantly, he'd discovered that true awareness isn't about being more observant, it's about understanding what your observations actually mean.

Jamie's reality check

But Jamie's early confidence would soon teach him a crucial lesson about the difference between beginner's luck and genuine mastery.

Three weeks on, Jamie felt unstoppable. Time to tackle the new literacy assessment policy with his newfound awareness skills.

He opened the staff meeting acknowledging that changes could be stressful, then explained the requirements in detail. As he spoke, he watched for the signs he'd learned to read. Perfect, heads were nodding, eye contact was maintained, no one was checking their phone. When he asked, "Any concerns?" silence. When he checked, "Does this make sense?" several yeses.

"I walked out feeling like I'd mastered this leadership thing," Jamie told me during our next mentoring session, his usual confidence notably deflated.

Forty-eight hours later, his assistant principal, Angela, delivered the brutal truth: "That meeting was a disaster. The teachers are furious. Those weren't nods of agreement. They were nods of resignation! Three teachers want transfers!"

Jamie's early success had created dangerous overconfidence. He'd confused compliance with consensus, politeness with buy-in. The nodding meant, 'I hear you,' not 'I agree with you'. The silence after, 'Any concerns?' wasn't satisfaction. It was resignation that their input wouldn't matter anyway.

"I learned that body language without context is meaningless," Jamie reflected. "Nodding can mean agreement, resignation, or politeness. I was projecting my hopes onto other people's behaviour."

This failure drove Jamie to develop his four-layer room reading approach: what's being said, what's the backstory, do words match body language, and what do these people need. More importantly, it taught him that awareness without understanding is just sophisticated guessing.

"Sometimes the most valuable thing that can happen to a leader is discovering you're not as good as you think you are," Jamie concluded.

This humbling experience shaped how Jamie approached the systematic development of his strategic empathy skills.

Two ways to respond when things get tense

When you hit resistance or confusion, and it's inevitable you will, you have about two seconds to decide how to respond. I've seen this choice point thousands of times, and it determines everything that happens next.

Push through: "We need to move forward regardless. Here's what we're doing." This might get compliance if you have enough authority, but it rarely gets commitment. And in today's workplace, compliance without commitment doesn't build effective workplace culture.

Pause and explore: "I'm sensing some concern here. Help me understand what's not working." This approach takes maybe a minute longer, but it gets you genuine buy-in. More importantly, you often discover information that makes your original plan better.

Watch for these critical moments as they happen in every important conversation: when someone offers a different view that challenges your plan, when the energy in the room suddenly shifts, when a quiet person finally speaks up, or when frustration or excitement becomes visible.

Your response in these moments often determines whether you get collaboration or compliance, whether problems get solved or just postponed.

What to say when you spot the triggers

When you recognise these trigger points, having the right words ready makes all the difference. Here's what to say in each situation.

When people feel bulldozed, try something like, "Help me understand how you see this" or "What would need to change for this to work better?" You could also say, "I value your experience here. What am I missing?"

These responses show you're genuinely interested in their perspective rather than just pushing your agenda.

If someone seems confused, it's usually better to acknowledge your role and say, "Let me be clearer about what I mean" or ask, "What questions do you have that I haven't answered?"

Sometimes it helps to check your assumptions with, "How are you interpreting what I just said?"

When people feel unsettled by what you're proposing, acknowledge that directly. Try, "This is a big change. What feels most concerning?" or "What would you need to feel confident about this?" You might also ask, "How can we make this transition easier?"

The key is recognising that feeling unsettled is normal and giving people space to work through it rather than rushing them past their concerns.

The 3-minute meeting reset

When things go sideways, and they will, try this approach.

In the first minute, say, "I'm noticing some tension here. That tells me we need to slow down for a moment."

In the second minute, ask, "What am I missing? What concerns haven't we talked about yet?"

In the third minute, redirect with, "Right, given what we've just heard, how do we move forward in a way that actually works?"

This isn't about being touchy-feely. It's about being smart. Deal with the emotional issues so you can actually solve the practical problems.

The pattern's always the same: acknowledge the emotional reality first, then tackle the practical challenge. It feels counterintuitive if you're used to just pushing through problems, but it works consistently.

Five immediate actions for your next meeting

Rather than trying to remember complex frameworks, focus on these simple interventions that create immediate improvements.

Ask how people are feeling: "How is everyone feeling about where we've landed?" Then actually listen to the answers. This simple check often reveals concerns that would otherwise surface as resistance later.

Notice who's not talking: If someone has gone quiet, try, "Gayle, I haven't heard your thoughts on this yet." Often the most valuable insights come from people who need explicit invitation to contribute.

Check the room's energy: If it feels drained, ask what's causing it. Energy levels tell you more about engagement than words alone.

Test for clarity: "Just so we're all aligned, here's what I think we've decided..." This prevents those frustrating "I thought you meant..." conversations later.

Surface concerns: "What problems might we hit with this plan that we should talk about now?" Better to address potential issues when you can still adjust course.

None of these are big dramatic interventions. They're tiny adjustments that create much better outcomes. The key is consistency and using these approaches regularly until they become natural responses rather than conscious techniques.

Making it stick: Building the habit

Reading about these approaches is the easy part. Actually implementing them when you're stressed, running late, and dealing with difficult people requires building new habits systematically.

Start with just one trigger you'll focus on this week. Don't try to fix everything simultaneously. Pick either power triggers, message gaps, or change shock and really notice when it shows up.

Block fifteen minutes daily for practice and diligently put it in your calendar, otherwise it won't happen. Each morning, ask yourself, "What tricky conversations am I likely to have today, and how do I want to handle them?"

During the day, pause occasionally to wonder, "What am I noticing here that others might be missing?" Then each evening, reflect on, "What patterns keep showing up? What's working? What isn't?"

This should only take about five minutes and can transform how you handle difficult situations.

Find someone you trust to give you feedback on changes in how you communicate. Most importantly, notice your wins. When you successfully navigate a tricky conversation, acknowledge it rather than immediately moving on to the next challenge.

You'll know it's working when you see real changes in your environment. More people start contributing in meetings. Those frustrating 'I thought you meant...' conversations become far less frequent. Problems get raised earlier rather than at crisis point. People leave your meetings energised rather than drained.

In a follow-up mentoring session, Jamie shared the improvements he'd seen just from asking better questions when he noticed changes in body language around the room.

"At first it was really hard," he admitted. "People weren't used to someone actually acknowledging what was really happening. They'd got so used to pretending everything was fine that when I started naming the tension or confusion, it felt uncomfortable for everyone."

That initial discomfort is completely normal. You're changing communication patterns that have been in place for years. People need time to adjust to a leader who actually pays attention to what's beneath the surface.

But Jamie stuck with it, and the results followed. His staff meetings went from being polite but unproductive gatherings into genuine problem-solving sessions where real issues got addressed before they became crises.

Your next step

This awareness you're building is the foundation for everything that follows. In Chapter 6, we'll explore how these individual moments of insight become systematic pattern recognition, allowing you to anticipate conversational dynamics rather than just react to them.

But that's next time. For now, pick one thing from this chapter and try it in your very next conversation with another human being. Not next week, not when you have time to prepare, but today.

Trust me, you'll be amazed what you notice when you start paying attention. And here's what's even more powerful: after a few weeks of building this awareness, you'll start noticing something interesting. The same situations keep appearing. The same triggers keep surfacing. The same responses keep working or failing. What seemed like random workplace chaos is following predictable patterns, which you can learn to anticipate and influence.

Key Takeaways: Trigger points

Conversations are icebergs: 20% visible words, 80% hidden emotions. Read all four layers: what's said, backstory, word/body alignment, and what's needed.

The Big Three Killers: When people feel bulldozed, confused, or unsettled, conversations die. Spot the warning signs early.

Choose your response: Push through and get compliance, or pause and explore to get commitment. You have two seconds to decide.

Use the reset: Acknowledge tension, explore concerns, redirect productively when things go wrong.

Try five things today: Check feelings, notice quiet voices, read energy, test clarity, surface concerns.

Start small: Pick one trigger to focus on, practice daily, get feedback, celebrate wins.

Trust the process: Awareness leads to recognition, recognition enables response, response builds habits, habits create your leadership signature.

6: THE LEADERSHIP MATRIX: SEE WHAT OTHERS CAN'T

In Chapter 5, you developed your leadership sixth sense, which is the ability to read individual moments and conversations with unprecedented clarity. You learned to spot the emotional landmines before they exploded, to recognise the golden moments when everything could change. But here's what happens next: those isolated insights begin revealing something far more powerful.

What if every leadership frustration you've endured - the team member who derails every meeting, the resistance that kills your best initiatives, the conflicts that drain your energy - aren't random acts of workplace chaos but **predictable patterns** following scripts you can learn to read and rewrite[1].

These patterns repeat because they're driven by underlying beliefs, unspoken fears, and invisible team dynamics that most leaders never see. Once you recognise them, you stop reacting to surface behaviors and start addressing the root causes that drive them. You begin to notice that resistance always emerges at the same point in change initiatives, that certain conversations consistently escalate in predictable ways, that your team's energy drops when specific triggers appear. This is pattern recognition in action - the bridge between isolated awareness and systematic leadership mastery.

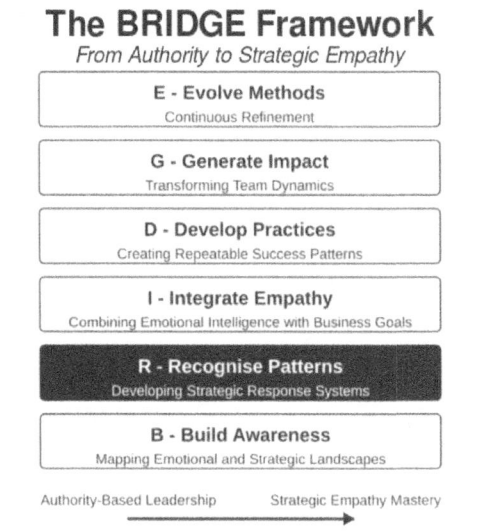

The BRIDGE Framework shows 'Recognise Patterns'. Having built awareness, you now develop the ability to connect individual insights into recurring patterns.

This shift from reactive management to strategic leadership liberates you from the endless cycle of solving the same problems over and over, having the same difficult conversations repeatedly, watching the same conflicts resurface no matter what you do.

You know that weight of walking into your office each morning carrying yesterday's unresolved tensions, knowing today will likely create new ones. That hollow ache when you realise your team's respect is eroding because you keep getting caught off guard by dynamics a more skilled leader would have navigated effortlessly.

Pattern mastery doesn't just give you better outcomes; it gives you back your nights, your weekends, your confidence that you're actually suited for this role. You stop being the leader who reacts to workplace chaos and become the one who creates workplace harmony. You become the leader who creates the leadership operating system that runs in the background, automatically detecting opportunities and threats.

When workplace chaos becomes workplace choreography

Every workplace runs on two systems. The visible one includes organisational charts, processes, and policies. The invisible one, which actually determines success or failure, consists of human patterns so predictable they might as well be code[2]. Most leaders spend their careers fighting the visible system while remaining completely blind to the invisible one.

Jamie, the principal I've been mentoring, came to our session three months later expressing confidence in how well he was managing interactions with staff. He was excited to share what had happened during a recent school council presentation about a new teaching methodology he hoped to introduce.

"I walked into that room and I knew it would all be OK," he told me. "Instead of feeling anxious about their reactions, I could actually see the patterns unfolding."

He described how he noticed the treasurer's slight frown when technology costs were mentioned, exactly as he'd expected. The parent representative's phone glance during policy discussions, right on schedule. The school council president's finger tapping, which Jamie now recognised as the reliable signal of concern about implementation.

But here's what had changed since our earlier mentoring conversations: Jamie no longer just reacted to these signals. He worked with them.

"I timed my response perfectly," he explained. "I said, 'I know we're all thinking about budget constraints. What if I told you this methodology could actually reduce our long-term training costs while improving student outcomes?' I could see everything shift in real time."

The transformation was instant. The frown disappeared. The phone went away. The tapping stopped.

As Jamie shared this story, I could see he'd mastered something powerful: pattern recognition isn't just about seeing what's happening, but influencing what happens next. When you learn to read these predictable responses, your biggest leadership frustrations transform into your greatest opportunities.

Finding your success formula

Here's something most leaders never do: they don't study their own wins. They celebrate briefly, then move on to the next challenge, completely missing the goldmine of insight buried in their success.

During my leadership, when I finally started investigating why some difficult conversations with staff succeeded while others crashed, I discovered something important. In heated moments when emotions were running high, my wins weren't luck. They followed a pattern I had unconsciously developed: I would pause and take a visible breath, giving everyone a moment to reset. Then I'd ask myself, "What's really driving this concern?" to get beneath surface positions. Finally, I'd align everyone around what success looked like for each person involved. This sequence worked consistently when I applied it deliberately.

But here's the breakthrough insight: my pattern was unique to me. It reflected my personality, my team's dynamics, and my organisational context[3]. No leadership book could have taught me this formula because it emerged from my specific leadership fingerprint.

Your success patterns are equally unique and equally powerful. They're hiding in plain sight, waiting to be decoded and deliberately applied. The difference between good leaders and extraordinary ones isn't talent or charisma but the willingness to become a detective of your own effectiveness[4].

Think about your last leadership triumph. Not the big promotion or strategic win, but that moment when a difficult conversation turned around, when resistance melted into collaboration, when confusion transformed into clarity. What specifically did you do? What sequence of actions created that result? What pattern can you extract and deliberately replicate?

This isn't academic analysis but your leadership DNA waiting to be discovered and systematically deployed. Understanding your success patterns builds confidence in high-stakes moments and stops you copying other leaders' styles that don't fit. This awareness doesn't constrain your authenticity - it amplifies your most effective self when it matters most.

Rewriting the resistance script

My friend Sofia's revelation changed everything about how she approached change management. As an HR director, she'd been treating each policy implementation as a unique challenge, crafting different strategies for every initiative. The results were exhausting and inconsistent.

When we caught up over coffee recently, she shared her breakthrough discovery. "I finally realised that resistance wasn't random but was following a script," she told me. "First confusion: 'What does this actually mean?' Then scepticism: 'Why are we really doing this?' Finally, either acceptance or rebellion. The same three-act play, performed by different actors, on different stages."

But Sofia's genius wasn't just in recognising the pattern but in realising she could rewrite the script. Instead of reacting to resistance, she began anticipating and addressing each act before it fully developed. Clarity before confusion could take hold. Compelling rationale before scepticism could flourish. Collaborative problem solving before rebellion could organise.

The transformation was profound. Policy changes that previously took months with grudging compliance now happened in weeks with genuine buy-in. Sofia hadn't changed what she was implementing; she'd changed how she navigated the inevitable human response patterns.

This is what I call moving from reactive problem solving to proactive pattern navigation. You stop fighting the current and start using it to reach your destination faster.

Your pattern laboratory

The most powerful leadership development tool isn't complex software or expensive coaching; it's a simple notebook and five minutes of daily reflection. This becomes your pattern laboratory, where abstract insights transform into concrete capabilities. Each day's entry captures not just what happened, but how you responded under pressure, which decisions energised your team, and where your natural instincts led you astray. Over weeks and months, these scattered observations reveal both your superpowers and blind spots.

During one of our mentoring sessions, Jamie shared a discovery that had saved him months of frustration. "I started tracking something interesting," he said. "I noticed that my staff members became defensive whenever I offered solutions before acknowledging their expertise. But when I reversed the sequence, putting acknowledgement first and solutions second, the resistance didn't just decrease, it disappeared entirely."

This wasn't theoretical leadership wisdom but personalised intelligence that emerged from paying attention to what actually worked in his specific context with his specific team. No two leaders will discover identical patterns because no two leadership contexts are identical.

I encouraged Jamie to capture four essential elements in his pattern laboratory: what triggered each interaction, how he responded, what the outcome was, and what pattern he was beginning to recognise. Over time, these brief notes revealed the invisible architecture of his leadership effectiveness.

The magic happens when you begin testing and refining these patterns deliberately. What seems random becomes predictable. What feels chaotic becomes manageable. What appears complex becomes elegantly simple.

The pattern traps that can derail you

Pattern recognition creates tremendous power, but power misapplied becomes weakness. I've seen leaders make three common mistakes that can completely undermine their progress.

The first trap is assuming one successful pattern works everywhere[5]. I watched this happen with one of my school leaders who discovered a questioning technique that transformed his relationship with his most challenging team member. Excited by this success, he applied the identical approach to everyone, creating confusion with some colleagues and resentment with others. "I thought I'd found the magic formula," he reflected later, "but I was treating different people like they were the same person." Each person and situation require its own approach - there's no 'cookie cutter' solution that works universally.

The second trap is seeing only what you expect to see. We naturally look for evidence that confirms our initial impressions while ignoring information that contradicts them[6]. True pattern recognition demands intellectual humility and actively looking for evidence that challenges your assumptions.

The third trap is overthinking when you should be responding. Some leaders become so focused on identifying the exact pattern that they miss the window to respond effectively. Pattern recognition must enhance your responsiveness, not replace it[7].

The solution isn't perfect pattern recognition, but pattern recognition combined with wisdom, humility, and good timing.

When patterns become second nature

Melanie's transformation from reactive firefighter to strategic leader began with a simple realisation: leadership excellence isn't built in dramatic moments but in everyday practices that build up over time.

"I used to believe leadership was about rising to big occasions," Melanie explained. "But the real breakthrough came when I realised that big occasions are determined by hundreds of small moments I'd been ignoring."

Her daily practice became beautifully simple yet powerful. Each morning, before checking emails or diving into urgent tasks, she invested five minutes asking herself three questions: "What conversations might unfold today? What patterns should I watch for? How can I prepare to respond thoughtfully rather than just react?"

Throughout the day, after important interactions, she captured brief observations in a small notebook: What happened? What worked? What pattern am I noticing? Before leaving work, she completed the cycle with three more questions: "What patterns emerged today? What responses proved most effective? What do I want to experiment with tomorrow?"

This wasn't complicated analysis but strategic reflection that gradually became unconscious competence. Within eight months, Melanie's team productivity increased, conflicts became rare rather than routine, and her own stress levels plummeted.

But the most profound change was qualitative: "I stopped feeling like leadership was happening to me and started feeling like I was actively creating my leadership experience."

Another leader I mentor, Tom, discovered his own pattern around team meetings. "I noticed that whenever I started meetings by asking how everyone was feeling about our current projects, the whole dynamic changed," he told me. "People opened up about real challenges instead of just giving status updates. We started solving problems instead of just reporting them."

Tom's insight led him to completely restructure his approach to team communication. Instead of agenda-driven meetings, he created space for genuine dialogue. The results spoke for themselves: timelines improved, team engagement soared, and the quality of solutions increased dramatically.

These leaders understood something crucial: pattern mastery transforms leadership from crisis management to strategic influence of workplace dynamics.

From pattern recognition to real results

Pattern recognition transforms leadership from art to science, from intuition to system, from hope to predictability. But the ultimate goal isn't just seeing patterns; it's leveraging them to create outcomes that seemed impossible through traditional authority-based approaches[8].

Tom exemplifies this transformation. Initially sceptical about whether 'soft skills' could address his school's escalating student behaviour issues, he reluctantly agreed to track concrete metrics: incident reports, suspension rates, and repeat offences. By the end of the semester, the numbers told an extraordinary story of substantial improvements across every measure, translating to significant time savings for staff and dramatically improved school climate.

"The data was compelling," Tom told me, "but the real transformation was emotional. We stopped dreading difficult students and started seeing them as pattern recognition opportunities. Each challenging behaviour became a chance to understand what was really driving the issue rather than just applying consequences."

His breakthrough came when he realised that most behaviour problems followed predictable patterns. Students acting out during certain subjects, particular times of day, or specific social situations. Instead of reacting to each incident individually, Tom's team began identifying triggers and addressing underlying causes proactively.

This shift from punishment to prevention, from reaction to understanding, from chaos to systematic intervention is what pattern recognition mastery delivers. You don't just become a better leader; you become a different kind of leader entirely[9].

What comes next

Pattern recognition shifts you from being blindsided by workplace drama to anticipating and influencing breakthrough moments. You move from damage control to outcome creation.

The leaders we've encountered (Jamie working with school council dynamics, my own experience with a success formula, Sofia rewriting resistance scripts, Melanie transforming daily practice, Tom shifting from reactive discipline to proactive intervention) demonstrate that pattern recognition isn't just another leadership skill. It's a fundamental shift in how you experience leadership itself.

But this is where many leaders encounter a frustrating paradox that prevents them from further developing their leadership operating system. You've built this incredible ability to read situations and understand people's underlying motivations with remarkable clarity. You know exactly what makes certain people react defensively and what drives others to resist change instinctively. You can sense how discussions will unfold before they've properly started.

Then comes the question that exposes leadership's most paralysing trap: "Right, so what do we actually do? Do we proceed or find ways to work around their resistance?"

Suddenly, all that insight feels completely pointless. You're staring at what seems like an impossible decision: show understanding and risk appearing weak or stay focused on results and risk seeming ruthless. Acknowledge their concerns and potentially derail progress or maintain direction and potentially destroy relationships.

This is the critical moment where most leaders get caught in what they assume is leadership's fundamental trade-off. They treat their enhanced awareness as merely a tool for better understanding people, completely missing what it's actually designed to unlock.

You've learned to see the matrix. Now we'll discover how to reshape it.

Pattern recognition gives you the map, but integration gives you the vehicle.

In our next chapter, we'll explore how to bridge what often feels like an impossible gap between understanding and action, between insight and influence. You'll discover why the empathy versus strategy dilemma isn't just false, it's backwards. The most strategically successful leaders aren't those who suppress empathy to make tough decisions; they're those who use empathy to make better decisions.

As we continue the journey you will learn how this integration transforms strategic empathy from an interesting concept into a competitive advantage that simultaneously builds trust and delivers bottom line impact. You'll stop choosing between being understanding or being effective and start discovering how to be both, simultaneously and authentically.

Let's start.

Key Takeaways: The leadership matrix

Two systems run every workplace: Visible systems (org charts, policies) and invisible systems (human patterns). Master the invisible one to truly lead.

Your success follows patterns: Your best wins contain your leadership DNA. Study them like a detective studies evidence as they are your unique formula for success.

Resistance follows scripts: Stop reacting to resistance and start anticipating it. Address each predictable stage before it fully develops.

Daily practice compounds: Five minutes of morning intention plus brief interaction notes plus evening reflection equals leadership transformation over time.

Avoid the pattern traps: Don't apply the same solution everywhere, don't see only what you expect, and don't overthink when you should act.

From chaos to influence: Pattern mastery transforms leadership from crisis management to strategic influence of human dynamics.

7: THE INTEGRATION CODE: WHERE EMPATHY MEETS STRATEGY

You've cracked the code. After mastering the pattern recognition principles in Chapter 6, you can now read workplace dynamics like a conductor reads sheet music by anticipating every crescendo, every discord, every moment when the orchestra might fall apart or create something beautiful.

But here's where most leaders hit a wall.

You're sitting in that quarterly review, armed with perfect pattern recognition. You can see exactly why Pauline shuts down whenever budget cuts are mentioned because it's the same protective response she showed during the last restructure. You understand precisely what drives Michael's resistance to the new client management system. His fear of looking incompetent mirrors the pattern you've observed in every tech rollout. You've read the room's emotional temperature with surgical precision.

And then the CFO asks the question that exposes leadership's biggest trap: "So what's your recommendation? Do we move forward or accommodate their concerns?"

Suddenly, your brilliant pattern recognition feels useless. You're faced with what seems like an impossible choice: be empathetic and risk being seen as weak or be strategic and risk being labelled as heartless. Show understanding and compromise results or drive outcomes and damage relationships.

This is the moment where most leaders believe they must choose sides in leadership's most destructive false dilemma.

What if everything you've been taught about this choice is wrong?

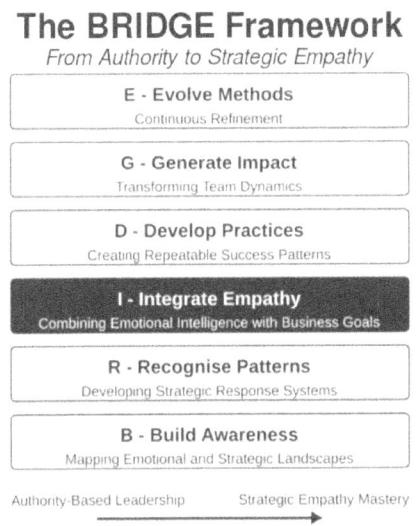

'Integration' forms the strategic core of The BRIDGE Framework, where emotional intelligence and business objectives unite to create purposeful leadership action. This critical component transforms empathy from a soft skill into a competitive advantage that drives measurable results.

When insight meets action: Jamie's integration moment

Jamie discovered this wall during what should have been a routine school council meeting several months after our pattern recognition breakthrough. He could see exactly why Margaret, the long-serving council member, would resist the new literacy programme. Her defensive posture whenever evidence-based educational research was mentioned had become as predictable as sunrise. He understood precisely what drove Robert's scepticism about budget allocations.

Jamie had read the room's emotional temperature perfectly. Then the school council president asked the question that exposed leadership's biggest trap: "So what's your recommendation, Jamie? Do we move forward with this programme or accommodate their concerns about the budget?"

"I felt like I had all this insight but nowhere to put it," Jamie told me during our next mentoring session. "I could see exactly what was happening, but I didn't know how to use that understanding to actually move things forward."

That's when I shared something with Jamie that changed how he thought about leadership entirely. The leaders who truly excel have discovered that empathy and strategic thinking aren't competing priorities but complementary powers that, when skilfully integrated, create outcomes neither could achieve alone[1].

This isn't feel-good theory.

But here's what makes integration so challenging: pattern recognition without the ability to act on it is like having perfect vision while wearing a blindfold. "I thought I had to pick a side," Jamie reflected during one of our coffee catch-ups. "Either I could be the understanding principal who listened to everyone's concerns and probably achieved nothing, or I could be the decisive leader who pushed through what needed to happen and probably damaged relationships."

Here's what I told Jamie: this is leadership's most persistent myth. You've been sold a lie that showing understanding somehow compromises your ability to make tough decisions. The most strategically successful leaders aren't those who suppress empathy to make tough decisions; they're those who use empathy to make better decisions[2].

Jamie's integration paralysis

But before Jamie could master true integration, he had to learn this lesson the hard way through a failure that nearly derailed his progress.

Six months into his strategic empathy journey, Jamie faced his biggest test yet: a serious safety incident involving a teacher's classroom management that put students at risk. Everything he'd learned about integration would be challenged.

"I thought I finally understood how to balance empathy with decisive action," Jamie told me during our emergency mentoring session that week. "Instead, I created a disaster by trying to be understanding and strategic at the same time."

When the incident occurred, Jamie's first instinct was to apply his integration framework. He called the teacher in for a meeting, determined to acknowledge her stress and personal challenges while addressing the safety concerns. But instead of finding the sweet spot between empathy and action, Jamie got paralysed trying to honour everyone's feelings.

He spent forty-five minutes exploring the teacher's perspective, acknowledging her recent divorce and workload pressures, validating her passion for students. Meanwhile, the safety issue remained unaddressed. When parents called demanding immediate action, Jamie asked for more time to 'work through this collaboratively'.

"I was so focused on not being the authoritarian principal that I stopped being a principal at all," Jamie reflected. "I confused integration with indecision."

The situation spiralled quickly. Parents lost confidence in his leadership, questioning whether he prioritised teacher comfort over student safety. The school council demanded a meeting. Even the teacher felt unsupported, interpreting Jamie's lengthy process as doubt about her competence rather than care for her wellbeing.

"I thought integration meant avoiding tough decisions," Jamie told me. "But all I did was delay an inevitable choice while making everyone lose faith in my judgement."

The wake-up call came when an experienced principal colleague pulled him aside: "Jamie, empathy without decisive action isn't leadership, it's therapy. Your job isn't to make everyone feel good about difficult decisions. It's to make the right decisions with emotional intelligence."

This failure taught Jamie that integration isn't about avoiding tough calls but making them with full awareness of their human impact. True strategic empathy means understanding all perspectives, then choosing the course that serves the larger good while minimising unnecessary harm[3].

"I learned that being decisive and being empathetic aren't opposites," Jamie concluded. "The most empathetic thing you can do sometimes is make the hard choice quickly, before uncertainty damages everyone involved."

The strategic pause that changes everything

Three months after that humbling experience, Jamie faced a similar situation with the school council debating a new student wellbeing programme. But this time, he was ready with what I call the strategic pause, which is a simple technique that transforms integration moments from obstacles into opportunities.

Here's exactly what Jamie did, and what you can do in challenging leadership moments.

When you notice that gap between what people are saying and what they're feeling, when someone's reaction seems too big for the situation, when good ideas hit unexpected resistance, that's your integration moment. Most leaders miss these entirely because they're focused on getting through their content. But once you start looking for them, you'll spot them everywhere.

The strategic pause[4] has three parts, and it takes about thirty seconds total. First, Jamie learned to absorb and assess both the emotional and strategic information simultaneously. Instead of immediately defending his proposal, he took a moment to consider what Margaret's research scepticism told him about implementation challenges, and what Robert's budget concerns revealed about sustainability issues.

Second, he learned to find where personal concerns and organisational goals overlap rather than conflict. This shift in perspective transforms leadership from a constant battle of wills into collaborative problem-solving. Instead of viewing motivations as threats to collective objectives, effective leaders discover the sweet spot where what people genuinely care about aligns with what the organisation needs to achieve.

This is where the magic happens.

Jamie stopped treating Margaret's scepticism as an obstacle to overcome and started seeing it as valuable input about programme credibility. He didn't see Robert's budget worries as resistance but as shared concern about getting it off the ground and its long-term viability.

Third, Jamie responded with integration, that is, crafting responses that honoured emotions whilst advancing objectives. To Margaret, he said, "Your experience with previous initiatives matters. Would you help us design evaluation criteria so we can measure whether this is actually working?" To Robert, he said, "You're right to question the budget. What if this programme could reduce our external counselling costs whilst providing better student support?"

The transformation was instant. Margaret volunteered to chair the evaluation committee. Robert offered to help model the financial projections.

"As I drove home that night," Jamie told me, "Something clicked that I hadn't expected. I wasn't exhausted like I usually was after difficult meetings. I felt energised. Then it hit me."

He paused, still amazed by his own realisation months later.

"For years, I'd been treating people's concerns as obstacles to overcome. That night I realised I'd been doing it completely backwards. Their concerns weren't roadblocks but rather the raw materials for better solutions. Margaret's scepticism about research made our evaluation process stronger. Robert's budget worries led to a more sustainable financial model."

Jamie leaned forward, eyes bright with the memory. "I literally pulled over to the side of the road because the realisation was so profound. I wasn't managing people despite their emotions. I was succeeding because of them. Every concern, every resistance, every difficult question was actually showing me how to build something better."

Finding where hearts and minds align

What Jamie discovered that night transformed his entire approach to leadership. He'd stumbled onto something powerful: the place where personal needs and organisational goals don't just coexist but actually strengthen each other.

Most leaders think they're facing a choice between being empathetic or being strategic. But Jamie learned to look for the overlap, the sweet spot where what people care about personally connects with what the organisation needs to achieve.

During our next mentoring session, Jamie described how he'd started approaching every challenging conversation differently. "Instead of seeing resistance as something to overcome, I started seeing it as information about how to make my ideas better," he told me.

When teachers expressed concern about a new instructional teaching model, Jamie didn't dismiss their worries or push through regardless. He asked, "What would need to be different about this approach for you to feel confident it would actually help your students?" Their concerns about workload led to a streamlined version that was more effective than his original proposal.

When parents worried about changes to the homework policy, Jamie didn't defend the policy or abandon it. He said, "I can see you're concerned about how this might affect your child's preparation for high school. Help me understand what success looks like from your perspective." Their input led to modifications that addressed their concerns whilst achieving the educational objectives.

The pattern was always the same: acknowledge the emotional reality, then use it to improve the strategic approach. "I stopped choosing between empathy and strategy," Jamie explained, "and started using empathy to make my strategy more effective."

What to say when you know what's really happening

The strategic pause gives you the framework but knowing exactly what to say in integration moments makes the difference between theory and practice. Jamie learned specific phrases that consistently turned resistance into collaboration.

When he noticed emotional resistance, instead of pushing through with logic, Jamie learned to say, "I can see this is concerning. Help me understand what's driving that concern."

This acknowledges the emotion whilst gathering strategic information about what's really causing the resistance.

If someone seemed confused or overwhelmed, rather than explaining more of the same thing, Jamie would say, "Let me step back and make sure I'm being clear about what this means for you specifically." Then he'd focus on their particular situation rather than repeating general information.

When facing scepticism about new initiatives, instead of defending the idea immediately, Jamie learned to ask, "What would need to be different about this approach for you to feel confident it could work?" This transforms scepticism into valuable design input.

For budget or resource concerns, he learned to acknowledge the constraint whilst exploring possibilities: "Given our budget realities, what would the minimum viable version of this look like?" This shows understanding of their limits whilst keeping the strategic objective alive.

When someone offered a different perspective that challenged his plan, instead of dismissing it, Jamie would say, "That's an important perspective. How could we incorporate that insight into what we're building?" This turns potential conflict into collaborative problem-solving.

"The important thing about these phrases is they felt genuine," Jamie told me. "I wasn't pretending to care about their concerns. I actually did care, because their concerns were showing me how to build something better."

Making integration your natural response

Integration becomes natural through consistent practice rather than occasional dramatic moments. Jamie developed five daily practices that gradually made empathy-strategy integration his default leadership approach.

Each morning, before checking emails or diving into urgent tasks, Jamie spends two minutes asking himself: "What challenging conversations might unfold today? How can I prepare to respond with both understanding and purpose?" This mental preparation means he's less likely to be caught off guard when integration moments arise.

During important conversations, Jamie learned to pause internally and ask himself, "What's happening beneath the surface here? What strategic opportunity might this reveal?" These quick check-ins keep him gathering complete information rather than just pushing through his agenda.

After difficult interactions, Jamie captures brief observations in a notebook. What emotions did people show? What strategic information did that provide? What worked well in his response? What would he do differently? This reflection turns experience into learning rather than just moving on to the next crisis.

Before making significant decisions, Jamie now involves the people who'll be affected. Not just to be nice, but because their input makes his decisions more effective. "What concerns do you have about this direction?" he asks. "How could we address those whilst still achieving our objectives?"

Each evening, Jamie spends five minutes reviewing the day. What integration moments did he handle well? Where did he default to old patterns of choosing either empathy or strategy? What does he want to practice tomorrow?

"The beautiful thing about these practices is they don't add time to my day," Jamie told me. "They just make the conversations I'm already having more effective."

Within six months, the results were measurable. Decision acceptance rates improved dramatically. Those frustrating 'I thought you meant...' conversations became far less frequent. Team contribution in meetings increased because people felt safe to share concerns and ideas. Problems got raised early when solutions were still possible rather than festering until they became crises.

When the pressure is on: Jamie's ultimate test

Jamie's ultimate test came twelve months later when the school budget revealed staffing levels would be affected. School council was split, parents were vocal in their views, teachers were threatening industrial action. Everything he'd learned about integration would be tested under maximum pressure.

High-stakes moments reveal whether integration has become genuine capability or just a nice-weather technique. When emotions run high and time pressure mounts, most leaders default to their old patterns, either pure empathy that avoids tough decisions or pure strategy that steamrolls over human concerns.

Jamie approached this crisis with integrated thinking from the start. He mapped the emotional landscape with the same precision he'd once applied to budget spreadsheets. Teachers were just as worried about job security as they were passionate about student outcomes and would support necessary changes if they believed those changes would ultimately benefit students. Parents weren't just demanding smaller class sizes. They also wanted assurance that their children's education wouldn't be compromised.

His solution emerged from finding where these different needs overlapped rather than conflicted. Jamie proposed a restructuring that combined classes strategically whilst creating specialist teaching roles that enhanced the educational programme. The cost savings came not from cutting positions but from using positions more efficiently.

The breakthrough happened at the very next school council meeting, which turned out to be a heated debate about the proposed changes. When angry parents demanded he protect their children from 'experimental changes,' Jamie didn't defend his proposal or dismiss their concerns. Instead, he said, "You're absolutely right that your children's education is too important to risk on untested ideas. That's exactly why we need your help to design this transition carefully."

He asked parents to join evaluation committees. He invited teachers to help design the new specialist roles. He turned the resistance into collaborative energy focused on making the restructuring work better rather than fighting whether it should happen at all.

The result was a budget solution that saved the required money whilst improving teacher job security and educational outcomes. Parent satisfaction increased. Teacher morale soared. School council approved the proposal unanimously.

"I operated simultaneously with understanding and effectiveness," Jamie reflected. "I didn't choose between heart and mind. I refused to choose at all."

Integration under pressure requires practice during calmer moments. You can't suddenly become empathetically strategic during a crisis if you haven't built that capability through daily practice. But when you have developed it, high-stakes moments become opportunities to demonstrate leadership that few others can match.

The integration of empathy with strategy isn't about finding balance between competing forces. It's about discovering a form of leadership power that most leaders never access because they believe they must choose sides in a false dilemma.

But here's what Jamie discovered next: knowing how to integrate empathy and strategy and doing it consistently when you're tired, stressed, and overwhelmed are two entirely different challenges.

The question that determines your leadership legacy

Jamie discovered what every exceptional leader eventually learns: knowing how to integrate empathy and strategy is only half the battle. The real challenge lies in making this approach so deeply embedded in your leadership DNA that it becomes your natural response, especially when you're tired, stressed, and overwhelmed.

"I want to build systems that work even when I don't feel like working the system," Jamie said during a recent mentoring session, articulating perfectly what every leader faces after their initial breakthrough.

You've spent your career being told that leadership requires tough choices. Jamie discovered that's the biggest lie ever sold to ambitious people. The most powerful leaders aren't those who pick sides between empathy and effectiveness. They're those who refuse to accept that these forces oppose each other.

When you master integration, you don't just become a better leader. You become a different kind of leader entirely. One who doesn't see resistance as an obstacle to overcome but as raw material for building something better. One who doesn't manage people despite their emotions but succeeds because of them.

But here's what separates great leaders from those who merely have great moments: the ability to make this integrated approach sustainable[5]. It's one thing to successfully navigate a difficult conversation when you're prepared and energised. It's entirely different to maintain that same level of strategic empathy when everything is falling apart and you're running on empty.

The question that will define your leadership legacy isn't whether you can apply these techniques when everything's going well. It's whether they become your default response when everything's falling apart.

That's the leader your organisation needs. That's the leader your team deserves. That's the leader you're capable of becoming.

The choice, or rather, the refusal to choose, starts now. But making it stick when the pressure is on? That's where we're heading next.

Key Takeaways: The integration code

Integration moments happen everywhere: Watch for when people's words don't match their body language, when reactions seem too big for the situation, and when good ideas hit unexpected resistance. These aren't problems to solve but clues about what's really happening.

The strategic pause has three simple steps: First, notice both the emotions and the business needs in play. Second, find where what people care about connects with what the organisation needs. Third, respond in ways that show you understand their concerns whilst still moving things forward.

The right words make all the difference: Try phrases like, "Help me understand what's worrying you about this," and, "What would need to change for you to feel good about this direction?" These show you care about their concerns whilst helping you learn what really matters.

Small daily habits create big changes: Start your day thinking about tricky conversations ahead, check how people are feeling during important discussions, reflect briefly after difficult interactions, involve people in decisions that affect them, and spend five minutes each evening noticing what worked well.

Pressure reveals your true leadership skill: Integration during calm times prepares you for crisis moments. When stress is high, skilled leaders channel resistance into problem-solving energy instead of falling back on either being too soft or too harsh.

Hearts and minds aren't opposites: The most powerful leadership happens when you find where personal concerns connect with organisational goals, turning resistance into the raw materials for better solutions.

8: BEYOND GOOD INTENTIONS: MAKING IT STICK

Jamie was convinced he had it down pat.

After mastering the integration breakthrough, his leadership confidence was soaring. School council meetings flowed with collaborative energy. Staff conflicts resolved within days. Parents praised his balanced approach. He walked the corridors with a spring in his step, greeting staff members who actually seemed pleased to see him coming rather than finding urgent reasons to duck into classrooms. The transformation felt almost magical - where once he'd dreaded difficult conversations, he now approached them with genuine curiosity about what he might discover. His assistant principal, Angela, commented that his office door stayed open more often, and the steady stream of complaints had been replaced by people seeking his input on creative solutions.

"I finally understand this strategic empathy thing," Jamie told me during what I assumed would be a celebration session. "I've got this."

Famous last words.

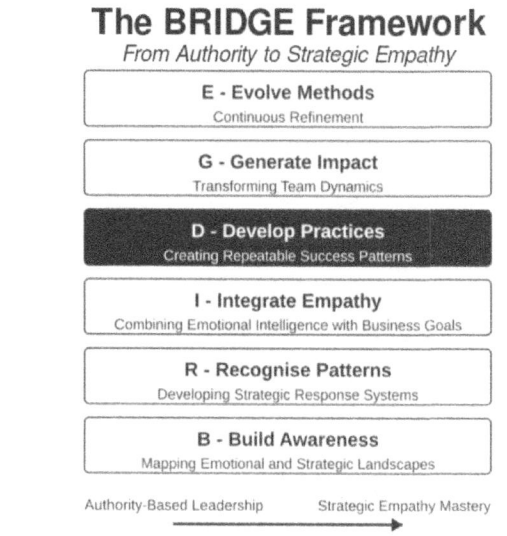

"Powerful conversations unfold through strategic empathy, not executive authority"

The BRIDGE Framework's 'Develop' component focuses on creating sustainable practices that ensure strategic empathy becomes your leadership default, not just an occasional aspiration.

Three weeks later, Jamie called me in crisis mode. A heated staff meeting had just imploded spectacularly. Despite months of practising his integration framework, he'd reverted to his worst habits the moment real pressure hit.

"All my integration techniques just... disappeared," Jamie said. "When that teacher challenged my decision about library hours, I didn't pause, I didn't integrate. I just shut her down like the old me used to do. Months of progress evaporated in six seconds."

Here's the brutal truth about leadership development: knowing what to do, and doing it when you're stressed and overwhelmed, are completely different skills.

You can master every technique in this book. But if those capabilities disappear the moment real pressure hits, you haven't built leadership skills, you've built performance art.

The gap between good intentions and consistent action is where most leadership development dies. It's the graveyard of brilliant frameworks that work perfectly in workshops but crumble under Tuesday afternoon reality.

What separates leaders who plateau from those whose impact compounds is the willingness to build systems that work especially when you don't feel like working the system.

The leaders who truly transform organisations aren't those who can apply these techniques when everything's going well. They're those who've made strategic empathy so automatic that it shows up precisely when it matters most, when the stakes are high, emotions are raw, and easy answers have been tried[1].

What you're about to discover

Most leaders focus on looking busy instead of being effective. They track vanity metrics - hours worked, meetings attended, emails sent - rather than outcomes that matter.

The real challenge isn't perfection under ideal conditions. It's maintaining your leadership standards when everything goes wrong: tight deadlines, difficult conversations, unexpected crises.

Your team doesn't need a flawless leader. They need a reliable one. They need someone whose decision-making process and communication style remain consistent regardless of external pressure.

The question is: are you ready to build something that actually sticks?

The failure that changes everything

That library meeting disaster became Jamie's most valuable leadership lesson. Instead of pretending it hadn't happened or making excuses, he did something that surprised everyone in the room, including himself.

He stopped the meeting.

"I need to restart this conversation," he announced. "I just did exactly what I've been working not to do, and Julie deserves better from me."

He acknowledged the teacher's concern about library access, admitted he'd felt threatened by her challenge, and asked her to help him understand what reduced hours would mean for students. The conversation that followed was one of the most productive they'd ever had, finding a creative solution that preserved most library access whilst meeting budget requirements.

But the real breakthrough came later that evening when Jamie dissected what had actually happened. His integration framework hadn't failed him; he'd simply abandoned it the moment stress spiked. Every technique he'd practised worked beautifully when he felt calm and in control. The cruel irony: his stress-management tools only worked when he wasn't actually stressed.

"I'd built systems for ideal conditions," Jamie realised, "not for when everything's falling apart and I'm running on fumes."

This failure taught Jamie the crucial lesson that sustainable leadership isn't about perfection. It's about building frameworks robust enough to work even when you don't feel like working the framework.

Building pressure-proof systems

Jamie began rebuilding his approach with one question: Will this hold up when I'm at my worst?

He started by mapping his patterns during those worst leadership moments. Staff meetings that rambled without purpose. Difficult conversations that spiralled into defensiveness. Decisions that dragged on because he overthought every variable. The common thread was improvisation. He was winging his way through predictable challenges.

"I was exhausting myself by reinventing solutions to the same problems," Jamie discovered.

His first target was staff meetings, which were at times mind-numbing obligations for everyone involved. His new system was elegantly simple: fifteen minutes for genuine check-ins where people could share real challenges, thirty minutes focused on one substantive issue that mattered to everyone, fifteen minutes planning concrete next steps with clear ownership.

Same people, same room, completely different energy.

With this conscious, deliberate and consistent approach, staff felt far greater satisfaction with how their weekly meetings ran. More importantly, Jamie found himself arriving at meetings energised rather than braced for endurance. The framework freed his mental energy for what really mattered: reading the room, connecting with individuals, spotting integration opportunities he used to miss whilst scrambling through agendas.

For difficult conversations, Jamie systematised his integration approach. The first and most important step was to assess both emotional and strategic landscapes simultaneously. Secondly, he had to work at finding where personal concerns and organisational goals overlap rather than conflict. It was only then that he could respond with integration, crafting solutions that honour emotions whilst advancing objectives.

But Jamie's masterstroke was creating what he called pressure protocols. These were specific reminders for high-stress situations when his best intentions collided with his worst moments.

A note on his desk: 'Acknowledge first, then integrate'. A phone reminder before difficult meetings: 'What does success look like for everyone in this room?' A card in his wallet: 'Pause. Breathe. What's really happening here?'

These weren't inspirational platitudes. They were emergency procedures for when willpower failed, and by noticing these constantly, they became embedded in his subconscious.

The goal wasn't rigid scripting but frameworks that make best practices automatic. When the technical elements run on autopilot, your humanity can show up fully for what truly matters.

Jamie stress-tested these systems during his next major challenge, which was a staff illness outbreak coinciding with unexpected issues with student behaviour and parent complaints escalating to the Department of Education. This time, something had fundamentally shifted.

Instead of reverting to command-and-control mode, he found himself instinctively applying his frameworks even under extreme pressure.

His pressure protocols kicked in automatically.

His meeting structure held firm despite the chaos.

And most importantly, his team noticed the difference and started seeking his guidance rather than avoiding him during the crisis.

The frameworks he'd practiced during calm moments became the foundation that held everything together when the stakes were highest. What had once felt like performance art - consciously choosing empathy over efficiency - now felt like second nature, allowing him to navigate multiple crises simultaneously without losing his emotional equilibrium. His colleagues later commented that he seemed more present and decisive during the chaos than he had ever been during normal operations.

The systems had transformed from conscious techniques into unconscious competence.

"The systems weren't just working," Jamie reflected. "They were working when I needed them most."

Measuring what moves the needle

But Jamie soon discovered that building robust systems was only half the challenge. Without proper measurement, he was flying blind, celebrating activity whilst his actual impact remained invisible[2].

"I was tracking how many meetings I held and emails I sent," Jamie admitted, "celebrating busy-ness whilst my leadership effectiveness stayed unmeasured."

Jamie learned to distinguish between vanity metrics and value metrics. Vanity metrics - emails sent, hours in meetings, policies written - made him feel productive but predicted nothing about success. Value metrics revealed actual leadership effectiveness such as voluntary collaboration between teams, speed of decision implementation, quality of ideas generated in meetings[3].

Jamie settled on four leading indicators that predicted school performance: meeting satisfaction scores, action completion rates, instances of voluntary collaboration, and student engagement metrics.

"Simple, measurable, and directly connected to what I was trying to achieve," he explained. "Better to track four indicators religiously than twenty sporadically."

But metrics only told Jamie what was happening, not why. He needed feedback systems that would reveal whether his strategic empathy was actually working or just feeling better to him.

What came next was the need to engineer psychological safety by deliberately designing interactions that made honest feedback feel genuinely safe and not risky[4]. When Jamie began modelling his own vulnerability, sharing his own leadership struggles, when he admitted he was still learning, it gave everyone permission to be honest about what wasn't working.

Jamie deliberately turned conversations from status updates to a way of receiving specific feedback. Instead of asking, "How are things going?" he asked questions such as, "What's one decision I made recently that you disagreed with? When have you seen me at my leadership best? What's something I do regularly that makes your job harder?"

Most importantly, Jamie learned to respond to difficult feedback with curiosity rather than defensiveness. The moment he started saying, "Tell me more about that," instead of, "Here's why I did it that way," everything changed.

The key insight: metrics tell you what's happening, but only truth-telling relationships reveal what to do about it.

Another hard lesson for Jamie was to avoid the temptation of trying to fix everything simultaneously. Instead, he decided to focus on one priority area: integration in difficult conversations. Not three areas. Not five. One.

"I looked for the recurring theme across all my feedback," he explained. "The biggest gap was between understanding what people needed and knowing how to respond in ways that honoured their emotions whilst still moving things forward."

Jamie was able to define success in observable terms: fewer repeat conversations about the same issues, faster decision implementation, increased voluntary collaboration. He created realistic timelines that acknowledged both urgency and the time genuine change requires.

The breakthrough came when Jamie established informal agreements with trusted colleagues to experiment with new approaches in their regular interactions. Angela became his primary practice partner, providing immediate feedback on what worked and what didn't during meetings.

These low-pressure rehearsals allowed him to refine his skills before high-stakes situations arose, building muscle memory for the moments when emotions ran highest and time was shortest.

Growth happened through the development of supportive relationships with mentors, peers, and team members who provided ongoing feedback and encouragement. These relationships created opportunities to repeatedly exercise his developing integration skills in low-stakes situations, making them second-nature before applying them where they mattered most.

When strategic empathy becomes your default

The real test came during Jamie's external review crisis. But this time, instead of managing each challenge separately, Jamie applied his integration framework systematically. He acknowledged review stress whilst focusing on improvement opportunities. He honoured staff concerns about needed changes whilst building stronger succession planning. He addressed parent questions whilst demonstrating strategic progress.

"What began as conscious effort gradually became natural response," Jamie reflected. "Strategic empathy wasn't something I did anymore. It was simply how I led."

But something even more remarkable happened. Jamie's approach became infectious.

When his assistant principal faced a difficult parent complaint, Jamie watched her naturally apply the integration framework of acknowledging the parent's frustration whilst focusing on student outcomes. She hadn't been trained in the technique; she'd absorbed it from watching Jamie model it consistently.

During a tense staff meeting about curriculum changes, instead of waiting for Jamie to manage the resistance, his leader of the English curriculum stepped in with perfect integration language: "I can see there are real concerns here. Help us understand what would need to be different for this to work in your classroom."

Jamie's school gradually transformed from a place where problems festered until they became crises into a learning culture where strategic empathy was the default response to challenge.

His journey proved that when you systematically develop strategic empathy as your leadership default, it doesn't just change how you lead, it changes how leadership happens around you.

But as Jamie settled into his role as a leader whose systems worked well and whose team flourished, a nagging question began to surface. During a casual conversation with Angela, his assistant principal, she asked, "What happens to all this if you're not here anymore? I mean, you've created something amazing, but it all seems to depend on you being present to model it."

The question hit harder than Jamie expected. He'd mastered strategic empathy as his personal default, but he was about to discover that personal mastery was only the beginning. The real test wasn't what he could achieve while present and engaged. It was what would continue to flourish in his absence.

The question that would define his next phase of growth was both practical and profound: How do you build leadership that doesn't need you to survive?

Key Takeaways: Beyond good intentions

Systems work when you don't: Build frameworks robust enough to function even when you're stressed, tired, or reverting to old patterns. Your leadership autopilot should engage precisely when your willpower fails.

Failure is essential data: The moments when you completely revert to old patterns aren't setbacks as they provide powerful information about where you need stronger systems and clearer triggers.

Pressure protocols save the day: Specific reminders for high-stress situations - notes, phone alerts, wallet cards - provide the split-second guidance that prevents breakthrough moments from becoming breakdown moments.

Vanity metrics deceive, value metrics reveal: Track team dynamics, collaboration quality, and relationship effectiveness rather than meetings held, or emails sent. Four indicators tracked religiously beats twenty tracked sporadically.

Truth-telling requires engineering: Psychological safety doesn't happen accidentally. Deliberately design interactions that make honest feedback feel safe rather than risky.

One focus yields maximum impact: Most change efforts fail because they try to fix everything simultaneously. Choose one priority area where focused effort will yield the greatest returns.

The ripple effect multiplies your impact: When you consistently model strategic empathy, your team naturally absorbs and applies these approaches, creating a culture of integration without formal training programmes.

9: BEYOND YOUR PRESENCE: BUILDING LEADERSHIP THAT LASTS

Jamie's transformation from reactive leader to someone who naturally integrated empathy with strategy definitely didn't happen overnight. But as he reflected on his journey, one question kept nagging at him, especially after his conversation with Angela.

"I've built something powerful here," Jamie told me during a recent session. "My team responds differently, conflicts resolve more naturally, and everything feels more... sustainable. But what happens to all this when I'm not here to model it anymore?"

It was a question that would fundamentally challenge everything Jamie thought he knew about leadership development. He'd mastered making strategic empathy his default response, but he was about to discover that personal mastery was only the beginning.

The real test of leadership isn't what you achieve whilst you're present. It's what continues to flourish in your absence. Real leadership isn't about being indispensable. It's about making yourself beautifully unnecessary[1].

Jamie's question haunted him for weeks: *What happens to all this when I'm not here to model it anymore?*

The answer came sooner than he expected, and it nearly destroyed everything he'd built.

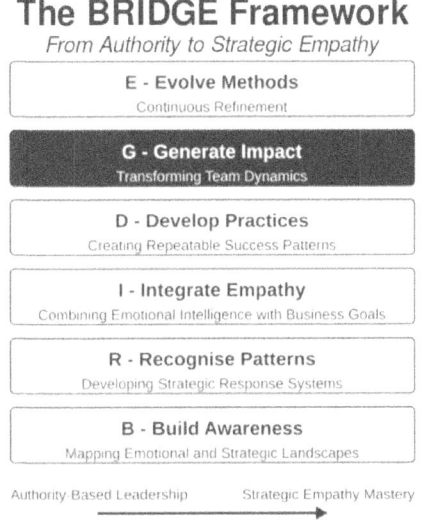

The BRIDGE Framework's 'Generate Impact' component focuses on creating leadership influence that multiplies beyond your presence through systems that think for themselves, wisdom that transfers to others, and cultural foundations that grow stronger over time.

The accidental experiment

Jamie's father had a stroke. Within 48 hours, Jamie found himself on indefinite compassionate leave, 200 kilometres away, watching his carefully cultivated leadership culture from a distance through anxious text messages and increasingly concerning phone calls.

Week one seemed promising. His assistant principal Angela stepped up magnificently, running meetings with the integration framework Jamie had modelled. Staff continued using the pressure protocols. The systems hummed along beautifully.

Week two, cracks started showing. Angela reverted to Jamie's old command-and-control style when tensions festered between staff. The maths leader ignored a difficult conversation rather than applying strategic empathy. Relationships were crumbling.

By week three, Jamie was receiving emergency calls from multiple staff members. "We need you back," became the constant refrain. "Nothing works without you here."

"I watched years of transformation evaporate in less than a month," Jamie told me during a crisis video call from his father's hospital bedside.

"Everything I thought I'd embedded was actually just me being present and working really, really hard."

Jamie had built a leadership culture entirely dependent on his personal energy and constant modelling. The moment he stepped away, the whole edifice collapsed.

"I'd created strategic empathy theatre," Jamie realised with devastating clarity. "People were performing it when I was watching, but they hadn't actually internalised it."

This brutal wake-up call forced Jamie to confront the hardest leadership question of all: *How do you build something that doesn't need you to survive?*

The dependency trap

When Jamie returned after six weeks, he found a school that had regressed further than he'd imagined possible.

Staff were avoiding difficult conversations entirely. Meetings had become status updates where people waited for direction. The collaborative energy had been replaced by anxious deference to authority.

"It was like watching a film rewinding," Jamie described. "Every behavioural change I thought was permanent had been revealed as conditional."

But Jamie's real shock came when he analysed what had actually happened. His staff hadn't failed to apply strategic empathy because they didn't understand it. They'd failed because they'd never learned to apply it independently of his presence.

"I'd been the strategic empathy engine for the entire school," Jamie admitted. "People knew how to follow my lead, but they had no idea how to lead themselves."

Jamie discovered he'd fallen into what I call the 'dependency trap', where your personal mastery becomes everyone else's limitation.

Instead of building leaders who could build other leaders, he'd built followers who could mimic leadership when supervised.

The wake-up call was painful but necessary. Jamie realised that sustainable transformation requires something far more sophisticated than good modelling and consistent systems. It requires leadership multiplication[2].

Building leaders who build leaders

"I had to completely rethink what development actually means," Jamie explained during our reconstruction session. "I'd been teaching people what to do rather than how to think."

Jamie's new approach started with a fundamental shift in perspective. Instead of being the strategic empathy expert, he needed to become the strategic empathy teacher. Instead of modelling perfect responses, he needed to develop the capacity of others to generate their own perfect responses.

He began with Angela, his assistant principal, but not in the way you might expect. Rather than giving her more responsibility, Jamie started giving her more decision-making authority in increasingly complex situations.

"I stopped rescuing her from difficult moments," Jamie explained. "When a parent complained aggressively about bullying, instead of stepping in with my integration framework, I asked Angela what she thought strategic empathy would look like in this situation."

The conversation that followed was messy, uncertain, and absolutely brilliant. Angela worked through the integration process aloud, acknowledged the parent's frustration whilst focusing on student safety outcomes, and found a solution that satisfied everyone involved.

"The difference was profound," Jamie reflected. "Angela hadn't just applied a technique. She'd developed the thinking behind the technique."

Jamie began to systematise this approach by creating deliberate and structured opportunities for staff to practice strategic empathy in real situations with coaching support rather than direct intervention.

During year level meetings where particular personalities often dominated, instead of facilitating integration himself, Jamie would identify emerging conflicts and asked: "How might you help everyone find common ground here?" Then he'd step back and provide feedback afterwards.

When discussions around student management became heated, rather than implementing his pressure protocols, Jamie would pause the meeting and ask: "What would strategic empathy look like right now?" Then he'd wait whilst the group worked it out together.

"I had to resist the urge to demonstrate competence," Jamie admitted. "Watching people struggle through problems I could solve instantly was genuinely painful. But that struggle was where the real learning happened."

The multiplication framework

Jamie's breakthrough came when he stopped thinking about strategic empathy as a skill to be taught and started thinking about it as a capacity to be developed.

He empowered his team through strategic coaching that built their capabilities from within.

He presented problems, not solutions. Rather than handing over ready-made answers, Jamie challenged his team with complex situations and guided them through the integration process, allowing them to demonstrate and develop their skills organically. This approach transformed team meetings into active problem-solving sessions where everyone contributed their expertise to finding solutions.

Jamie encouraged reflection on their thinking processes. By asking team members to articulate their reasoning and decision-making patterns, he helped them gain self-awareness without directly critiquing their choices. This approach fostered genuine learning rather than defensive reactions.

He shared perspective without prescribing action. Jamie offered his observations about situations while resisting the temptation to dictate specific responses. This created space for his team to draw their own conclusions and develop ownership of their decisions.

He embraced productive struggle. Most importantly, Jamie waited patiently for breakthrough moments, understanding that wrestling with challenges builds resilience and capability. He resisted the natural urge to rescue his people from difficulty, knowing that productive struggle leads to genuine growth and confidence.

Through this approach, Jamie moved his role from problem-solver to capability-builder, creating a team that could think independently and tackle complex challenges with confidence.

"It forced me to become comfortable with other people's learning curves," Jamie explained. "I had to trust that their messy, imperfect attempts at strategic empathy would eventually become their own elegant, authentic approaches."

The culture shift

The transformation became visible during Jamie's next planned absence, a two-week holiday he'd been dreading since his emergency leave disaster.

This time, something completely different happened.

Angela didn't revert to command-and-control leadership. Instead, she applied the learnings with her own team, helping them work through a complex literacy challenge using strategic empathy principles.

When a difficult parent meeting arose, Val, the school chaplain, didn't wait for direction. She used the peer coaching partnership to prepare, practiced integration language with her partner, and handled the situation independently whilst documenting the approach for others to learn from.

Most remarkably, when conflicts emerged, staff didn't avoid them or escalate them to leadership. They began applying strategic empathy spontaneously, helping each other find integration solutions in real time.

"I watched strategic empathy become the default response to challenge rather than an exceptional technique applied by exceptional people," Jamie marvelled when he returned to find the school functioning better than when he'd left.

"Strategic empathy had become how we naturally responded to pressure rather than something we tried to remember under pressure," Jamie realised.

When the framework walks without you

Liz and Chris were ready to tear each other apart over lab scheduling. Mathematics versus science. Territory versus access. The kind of departmental warfare that usually lands on the principal's desk with both sides demanding he choose a winner.

But Jamie never got the call.

Angela intercepted the conflict before it escalated. Not because she was told to, but because the multiplication framework had become her instinct.

"Before we make this Jamie's problem," Angela told Liz, "what's Chris actually trying to protect here?"

Liz's knee-jerk response, "Her precious science equipment."

"Probably," Angela agreed. "But if she's not just being territorial, what legitimate concern might be driving this?"

Twenty minutes later, Liz had mapped out Chris' real fear: mathematics groups were inadvertently disrupting carefully sequenced practical work that couldn't be easily rescheduled.

When Angela flipped the conversation with Chris, she discovered Liz's panic: intervention students needed predictable, hands-on learning environments, and irregular access was sabotaging the most vulnerable kids' progress.

Both were fighting for student outcomes. Neither could see it.

"What if," Angela suggested, "instead of fighting over the same space, we created something better?"

The solution that emerged - integrated STEM blocks where struggling maths students tackled real problems alongside science classes - solved everyone's problem while creating opportunities nobody had imagined.

Jamie learned about the resolution three days later.

"That's when I knew the framework had truly transferred," Jamie told me. "Angela hadn't just applied a technique. She'd become the kind of leader who sees conflict as raw material for innovation."

The ripple effect was immediate. Liz and Chris became strategic allies, their curriculum departments began collaborating spontaneously, and other staff started approaching conflicts as creative challenges rather than territorial disputes.

Strategic empathy had stopped being something they did when Jamie was watching. It had become how they naturally responded when nobody was watching at all.

Building your legacy system: when systems do the heavy lifting

Jamie built systems that made strategic empathy the lazy option. Here's what that actually looked like:

Meetings that couldn't help themselves - Every meeting started with: "What perspectives are we missing?" Not because Jamie demanded it, but because meetings consistently went south when they skipped this step. The two-minute investment saved hours of rework.

Meeting templates included: "What did we learn about each other today?" Strategic empathy became automatic, not an add-on training module nobody had time for.

Job descriptions with teeth - Jamie didn't add 'be empathetic' to job descriptions. He rewrote core functions, so empathy became essential. The literacy coordinator's role: 'Facilitate integration between classroom and specialist staff.' Translation: you can't succeed without understanding different perspectives.

Strategic empathy wasn't optional for excellence. It was required for competence.

The Three Lens Test - Any significant decision faced three questions: Student impact? Staff wellbeing? Community relationships? No decision moved forward without evidence all three were considered.

This wasn't bureaucracy. It was architecture that made empathy the fastest path to good decisions.

Performance reviews that counted - Instead of rating 'empathy' subjectively, Jamie measured its impact: How often do colleagues seek your input? How frequently do your interventions create collaborative solutions? How many innovations emerge from teams you facilitate?

These metrics made strategic empathy visible and valuable, not assumed and ignored.

New staff integration - New teachers got 'Integration Partners,' not policy handbooks. Within weeks, they experienced strategic empathy in action rather than hearing about it in orientation sessions.

Physical design that nudged connection - Jamie encouraged flexible group spaces. Noticeboards prompted: 'What's working in your area?', and 'What challenges could colleagues help solve?'

Environmental cues made collaboration feel natural, not forced.

The compound effect

Jamie's audit revealed the truth: strategic empathy language appeared in 89% of meetings without prompting. Peer partnerships formed spontaneously. When asked what made their workplace different, staff didn't mention policies; they talked about feeling genuinely heard.

"Culture isn't what you hope will happen," Jamie realised. "It's what you make inevitable through design. When strategic empathy becomes the easiest way to get things done, it becomes the way things get done."

The systems had replaced Jamie's presence. His legacy wasn't charisma; it was embedded structure that would outlast his tenure and keep evolving without him.

Jamie's experience taught him that sustainable leadership transformation requires three levels of development[3]:

Personal mastery: Developing your own strategic empathy capabilities until they become natural responses rather than conscious techniques.

Team multiplication: Building others' capacity to apply strategic empathy independently rather than just following your example.

Cultural embedding: Creating systems, structures, and stories that make strategic empathy the organisational default rather than depending on particular personalities.

"Most leaders stop at personal mastery and wonder why their impact dies with their tenure," Jamie reflected. "Real transformation happens when your best practices become everyone's normal practices."

The moment of truth

Jamie's journey from reactive crisis management to evolved leadership multiplication had prepared him for almost anything. His systems hummed, his culture thrived, and his strategic empathy had become beautifully automatic. But as he sat in his office one morning, staring at his calendar, he faced a sobering reality.

Three conversations this week would test everything he'd built: a performance review with his star teacher whose results had been slipping, an explosive conflict between two department heads that was poisoning team morale, and the devastating news about staffing cuts he had to deliver by Friday.

Six months earlier, any one of these conversations would have kept him awake at night. Now, something had shifted. These weren't disasters waiting to happen. They were opportunities to prove that strategic empathy wasn't just a nice idea. It was a leadership superpower that worked precisely when everything else failed.

"Here's what I've learned," Jamie told me during our session that week. "You can build all the systems you want, create the most empathetic culture imaginable, and evolve into the wisest leader in your field. But none of it matters if you can't handle the conversations that everyone else runs from."

Where theory meets reality

The brutal truth about leadership development is this: you're only as strong as your worst conversation. All your strategic empathy, all your evolved practices, all your multiplication frameworks, they mean nothing if you crumble the moment someone gets defensive, hostile, or devastated.

Those three conversations on Jamie's calendar weren't just administrative tasks. They were the final exam for everything he'd learned about leadership. They would reveal whether his transformation was genuine or just performance art that collapsed under real pressure.

But here's what separates leaders who plateau from those whose influence compounds exponentially: the recognition that difficult conversations aren't obstacles to great leadership. They're the raw material of great leadership.

The choice that defines everything

Every leader faces this moment. You can spend your entire career building elaborate systems to avoid the conversations that matter most. You can delegate the hard stuff, soften difficult messages into meaninglessness, and wonder why breakthrough opportunities keep going to someone else.

Or you can do what the most influential leaders throughout history have done: get dangerous.

Not reckless. Not harsh. Dangerous in the way that truth-telling is dangerous. Dangerous in the way that genuine care combined with unflinching honesty can transform everything it touches.

Jamie made his choice that morning. When his first difficult conversation arrived, he didn't avoid it, delegate it, or survive it.

He mastered it.

And in doing so, he discovered that the leader everyone respects, the one who gets the impossible results and builds the cultures others envy, isn't the one who avoids difficult conversations.

It's the one who has learned to use them as precision instruments for transformation.

Your most important conversation is waiting. When will you be ready to have it?

Key takeaways: Beyond your presence

'Strategic empathy theatre' reveals the illusion: When Jamie's emergency absence caused years of transformation to evaporate in weeks, he discovered people were performing empathy when supervised without actually internalising it. True development requires independent application, not just accurate imitation.

The dependency trap destroys sustainability: If your team needs you present to maintain strategic empathy, you've built followers who mimic leadership rather than leaders who generate solutions. Personal mastery becomes everyone else's limitation.

The multiplication imperative: Present problems not solutions, encourage reflection on thinking processes, share perspective without prescribing action, and embrace productive struggle over immediate rescue. This builds capability from within rather than dependence on external direction.

Systems make empathy inevitable: Meeting templates that ask, 'What perspectives are missing?', job descriptions requiring integration skills, and the Three Lens Test for decisions create architecture where strategic empathy becomes the easiest path to success, not an optional add-on.

Three levels of lasting transformation: Personal mastery gets you started, team multiplication creates independence, and cultural embedding makes strategic empathy the organisational default that survives leadership transitions.

The absence test defines legacy: Your leadership's true effectiveness isn't measured by what you achieve while present and modelling, but by what continues to flourish and evolve when you step away entirely.

Culture is what you make inevitable: When strategic empathy becomes embedded in structures, processes, and expectations, it stops being something exceptional people do and becomes how normal work gets done naturally.

10: THE SUCCESS THAT KILLS: WHY WINNING LEADERS LOSE THEIR EDGE

Towards the end of our mentoring relationship, I honestly felt Jaime had undergone profound learning over the many years we had worked together. I was confident he had reached the pinnacle of leadership mastery. He had transformed his school from low performing to exceptional. The Department of Education held it up as a model. Other principals sought his advice and now he was actively mentoring others. Five of his leaders had successfully gained promotions to other schools. His legacy systems hummed along perfectly, his culture thrived, and his team flourished.

That's why I was very surprised during what I expected to be a celebration session Jamie looked troubled. "Something's been bothering me for months. I can't shake the feeling that I'm... coasting."

"I started noticing it in small ways," Jamie explained. "My staff meetings followed the same patterns. My responses to conflicts had become predictable. Just last week, I caught myself giving the exact same feedback to a struggling teacher that I'd given to three others this term; not because it was the best response, but because it was my comfortable response."

This conversation would prove to be one of our most important. Jamie had stumbled into what I call the mastery trap, the dangerous illusion that leadership development has a finish line. It's the moment when your hard-earned competence becomes the enemy of your continued growth.

"The scariest part," Jamie continued, "isn't that I'm failing. It's that I'm succeeding so completely that I've stopped evolving. And in leadership, what feels like standing still is actually moving backwards."

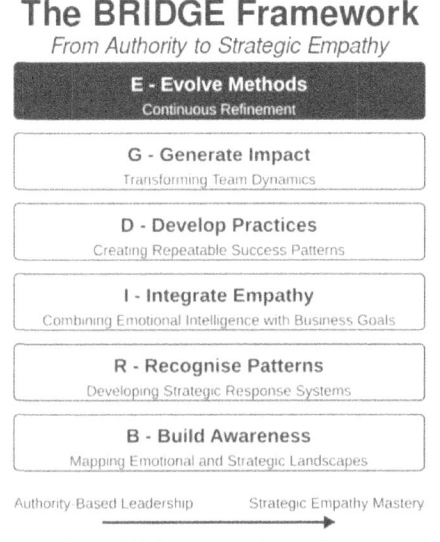

The 'Evolve and Adapt' element of The BRIDGE Framework helps leaders grow beyond their comfort zones by regularly checking how well they connect with others, actively seeking different viewpoints and quickly adjusting their approach to keep their leadership skills sharp.

When excellence becomes your enemy

The mastery trap doesn't announce itself with fanfare. It creeps in disguised as competence, wearing the mask of proven methods and reliable results. And you don't just wake up one morning and decide to stop growing. Instead, you gradually stop questioning whether there might be better ways to do what you're already doing well.

Here's the paradox that destroys more successful leaders than failure ever could: the moment you become truly excellent at something, you unconsciously begin optimising for proving you're right rather than discovering you're wrong. Excellence shifts your brain from learning mode to defending mode[1].

This realisation hit Jamie during a particularly unremarkable Wednesday afternoon staff meeting. As he listened to himself giving the same type of feedback he'd been offering for months, using phrases that had become comfortable patterns, he caught himself thinking, "When did I stop being curious about whether there might be a better way?"

"That question changed everything," Jamie told me. "I realised I'd fallen into exactly the trap I used to see in other leaders, believing that mastery was a destination rather than a journey."

Jamie remembered his earlier failures about the misread staff meeting where he'd confused compliance with consensus, the integration paralysis during the safety incident, the systems breakdown under pressure, and realised that complacency was just another trap waiting to catch successful leaders. Each previous failure had taught him something vital, but success was teaching him to stop questioning altogether.

Jamie's wake-up call

The moment that rocked Jamie's complacency came during a regional education conference. A newly appointed principal, barely two years into her first leadership role, presented an innovative approach to student engagement that made Jamie's 'best practices' look antiquated.

"Not wrong, not failing," Jamie reflected afterwards, "just... limited. I sat there thinking about all the conferences I'd stopped attending, all the books I'd stopped reading, all the fresh perspectives I'd stopped seeking."

That night, Jamie called me. "I've been so focused on perfecting what I know that I've stopped learning what I don't know. How did I become the kind of leader I used to criticise?"

This is precisely what I witnessed during my own 22-year journey as a school principal. After transforming my school from chaos to excellence, I fell into the same trap. The systems I'd created continued humming along efficiently, but something essential was missing, and it was growth.

"The view from the summit can be breathtaking," I shared with Jamie, "but if you stop climbing, you're actually moving backwards. In leadership, what feels like standing still is decline in disguise."

The evolution imperative

Here's what separates leaders who plateau from those whose impact continues expanding: the willingness to treat their current best as tomorrow's baseline. The leaders whose influence grows understand that in our rapidly changing world, yesterday's innovation becomes today's minimum standard[2].

When Jamie recognised he'd fallen into the mastery trap, he made a decision that felt counterintuitive: he would approach his next phase of leadership as if he were starting fresh. Not by abandoning everything he'd learned, but by rediscovering the curiosity that had made those early breakthroughs possible.

"I started doing things that felt uncomfortable again," Jamie told me. "I attended conferences outside education. I read a variety of autobiographies of successful leaders. I deliberately expanded my network to include new people who I knew would provide me with fresh and different perspectives. Most uncomfortably, I asked my newest and less-experienced staff members what they thought we could do differently."

This is what I call the evolution imperative, which is the recognition that continuous growth isn't optional but essential for sustained leadership effectiveness.

Building Jamie's leadership GPS

"I need a system," Jamie told me during our next session. "Something that prevents the comfort of success from becoming the enemy of growth."

Together, we developed what Jamie called his Leadership GPS, building on the measurement systems he'd previously established but now focusing specifically on how his strategic empathy practice itself was evolving. This wasn't just tracking outcomes anymore but tracking the continuous refinement of each BRIDGE component. The framework focused on three specific metrics that would sharpen his awareness, enhance his pattern recognition, and improve his integration capabilities[3].

1. Empathy accuracy

Jamie started logging his predictions about how people would respond to conversations, then comparing reality to expectation. "I was shocked," he admitted. "I thought I was reading people accurately, but I was wrong about 40% of the time."

During the period of conscious tracking, Jamie's accuracy rate began to improve instantly. More importantly, he discovered that his most significant leadership breakthroughs came from the moments when his initial read was wrong.

"The failures became my best teachers," Jamie reflected. "When my empathy assumptions proved incorrect, it forced me to dig deeper and discover what I'd missed."

2. Perspective diversity

Jamie began tracking how many different types of thinking he actively sought before making decisions. Not just more opinions, but genuinely different perspectives: operational, emotional, strategic, student-focused.

"I realised I'd been consulting the same people in the same ways," Jamie discovered. "My 'diverse' input was actually quite narrow. So I started deliberately seeking out contrarian views and fresh perspectives."

The impact was immediate. Jamie's decision-making improved noticeably as he incorporated insights from voices he'd previously overlooked.

3. Adaptation speed

Perhaps most revealing was measuring how quickly Jamie modified his approach when feedback suggested his initial empathy read was wrong. "In my early tracking, this often took weeks," he admitted. "I'd get feedback that my approach wasn't working, but I'd persist with minor tweaks rather than fundamental changes."

It didn't take long for Jamie to adapt within days or even hours. "The difference is that I stopped trying to perfect my current understanding and started measuring how quickly I could improve it."

Jamie's empathy evolution experiments

Every quarter, Jamie built experimentation into his routine operations, extending the practice partnership approach he'd developed earlier. Not major overhauls, but small tests that could fail safely whilst generating learning about how to enhance each element of the BRIDGE framework.

He experimented with meeting structures, tracking both efficiency and team satisfaction. "I discovered that most productive meetings happened when I asked better questions rather than providing more answers."

Jamie also tested approaches to difficult conversations, measuring both immediate outcomes and relationship quality. "I learnt that my instinct to solve problems quickly was actually preventing people from developing their own solutions."

He developed 'prediction practice' before announcing significant changes. He would privately forecast how team members might respond, then carefully observe their actual reactions during the announcement. He tracked not just verbal responses but also body language, the questions they asked, and concerns they raised afterward, comparing his predictions with reality to calibrate his understanding.

"Initially, I was right about 50% of the time," Jamie told me. "But the tracking itself made me more curious about what I was missing. It didn't take long for my accuracy to increase, and more importantly, my team felt truly understood."

The breakthrough that changed everything

Jamie's most significant breakthrough came when his empathy data revealed a blind spot he'd never recognised. He'd assumed that his most experienced teachers preferred autonomy and minimal guidance, whilst newer teachers needed more structure and support.

"The data showed I was completely wrong," Jamie laughed. "My experienced teachers actually craved more collaborative input on complex challenges, whilst my younger teachers wanted more independence to try their own approaches."

By tracking not just what his team did, but how they felt about doing it, Jamie discovered approaches that increased both effectiveness and job satisfaction.

"That's when I realised that evolution isn't just about personal growth," Jamie reflected. "The most powerful transformation happens when your evolved leadership becomes the foundation for transcendent impact on others."

Measuring what matters

"I needed proof that I was actually getting better at this, not just convincing myself I was," Jamie told me bluntly. "It's too easy to mistake feeling good about your empathy for actually being good at it."

Jamie's evolution practice demanded brutal honesty. He built on the metrics he'd established earlier - meeting satisfaction, action completion rates, voluntary collaboration - but now he was hunting for something deeper: whether his empathetic leadership was genuinely improving or just getting more comfortable.

He started tracking what he called his 'wrong rate', which was how often he completely misread situations. "This was incredibly humbling," Jamie admitted.

Who would have thought leaders who are wrong more often actually get better results, because they're gutsy enough to keep testing their assumptions instead of playing it safe.

Then came 'empathy lag time', how long it took him to realise his initial read was completely wrong and course-correct. "First quarter? Two bloody weeks on average. I was like a slow-motion empathy disaster. Now I'm pivoting within days, sometimes hours."

But the real test wasn't about Jamie. It was about his team. Were people actually speaking up more? Were fresh ideas surfacing? When conflicts erupted, were they getting resolved or just managed?

"The data didn't lie," Jamie said, leaning forward. "Better empathy accuracy meant better team performance. Seeking out voices that challenged me meant breakthrough solutions. Faster adaptation meant people trusted me more. It wasn't touchy-feely leadership theory. It was measurable impact."

Jamie's evolution legacy

Jamie's commitment to continuous evolution began to shift the dynamics around him in ways he hadn't anticipated. His assistant principal, noticing how Jamie handled criticism during their weekly planning meetings, started asking for similar feedback on her own leadership style. "If you can take Pauline's harsh feedback without getting defensive," she told him, "maybe I can learn to do the same with the team leaders."

"What surprised me wasn't some dramatic transformation," Jamie reflected. "It was how my willingness to be wrong gave others permission to be wrong too. When Robert saw that I could admit when my initial read of a situation was completely off, he started sharing his own uncertainties instead of just defending his positions."

The changes were subtle but meaningful. Team meetings became less about proving points and more about solving problems together. People began approaching Jamie with half-formed ideas, knowing he wouldn't judge them for thinking out loud or criticise them for wanting to share their ideas.

Jamie's journey from mastery trap to evolution mindset demonstrates a crucial leadership truth: your greatest competitive advantage isn't what you've already learned but your commitment to keep learning.

Your evolution roadmap

Breaking free from the mastery trap requires specific, measurable action focused on evolving your strategic empathy practice. Most leaders try to measure their empathy like they measure their performance, by tracking successes. The real breakthrough comes from measuring your empathy failures[4].

Start by establishing your own *'wrong rate'*- how often your initial read of situations proves incorrect. For the next month, write down your predictions about how people will respond to your communications, decisions, or changes. Then track what actually happens.

Next, create a ***perspective diversity scorecard***. Before making significant decisions, count how many different types of thinking you've actively sought. Not just more opinions, but genuinely different perspectives: operational, emotional, strategic, customer-focused.

Finally, measure your ***adaptation speed***. When you receive feedback that suggests your initial empathy read was incorrect, track how long it takes you to modify your approach. Set targets for reducing this timeframe.

Schedule monthly reviews of these metrics alongside your traditional performance indicators. What you'll discover is that improvements in empathy accuracy correlate directly with better team outcomes.

Create safe spaces for empathy experiments. Perform small tests of different approaches to reading and responding to team dynamics. Track both the immediate results and the learning generated.

Most crucially, treat your strategic empathy practice as a measurable skill that requires continuous refinement. The leaders who avoid the mastery trap don't just maintain their empathy; they systematically evolve it.

The choice that defines your legacy

Every successful leader faces this choice: rest on proven approaches or risk the discomfort of continued growth. The difference between leaders whose impact plateaus and those whose influence continues expanding isn't talent or opportunity but the willingness to remain permanently curious about the possibilities.

"The mastery trap is seductive because it offers the illusion of arrival," I told Jamie during our most recent session. "But the leaders whose stories inspire us decades later share one characteristic: they never stopped beginning. They treated each success not as a final destination but as a base camp for the next ascent."

Your legacy isn't defined by what you've already achieved. It's shaped by your willingness to keep evolving long after you've proven you know how to lead.

The edge you've earned through success? It's only as sharp as your commitment to keep honing it.

What comes next: From evolution to transcendence

Jamie's mastery of continuous evolution marked a pivotal moment in his leadership journey. "I thought the mastery trap was my final test," he told me during our most recent session. "But I've realised there is so much more to it."

As Jamie developed his Leadership GPS and embraced permanent curiosity, he discovered that evolved leadership opens doors to what I call transcendent impact, which is the ability to apply strategic empathy in the most challenging scenarios where traditional approaches often crumble entirely.

"The real test isn't whether you can evolve when things are going well," Jamie reflected. "It's whether your strategic empathy holds up when you're facing a crisis, delivering devastating news, or navigating conflicts that threaten to tear your team apart."

These words were uttered at what became our last mentoring session.

A few weeks later, Jamie was appointed to a regional position overseeing 300 schools, a role where everything he'd learned about strategic empathy would be tested on an entirely different scale.

But Jamie's story, powerful as it is, represents just one arena where strategic empathy transforms leadership.

The education sector, for all its challenges, operates within certain boundaries of shared purpose and collective mission. The corporate world, on the other hand, presents a different beast entirely, where bottom-line pressures, shareholder demands, and competitive markets create scenarios that would make Jamie's toughest school crisis look manageable.

This is where transcendent leadership truly proves itself. Not in the safety of aligned values, but in the crucible of conflicting priorities, impossible deadlines, and life-altering decisions that affect hundreds of careers with a single choice.

I discovered this when I met Kathy Chen, a CEO facing the kind of leadership crisis that breaks most executives. Her story would teach me that everything we'd learned about strategic empathy was just preparation for the real test - applying it when the stakes couldn't be higher and failure wasn't an option.....

Key takeaways: The success that kills

Success becomes the enemy: The moment you master leadership is when your leadership begins to decline. Excellence unconsciously shifts your brain from learning mode to defending mode, making you seek confirmation rather than growth.

Evolution requires measurement: Jamie's Leadership GPS tracked three key metrics: empathy accuracy, perspective diversity, and adaptation speed. What gets measured gets managed, especially in leadership development.

Wrong rates reveal wisdom: Leaders with the highest 'wrong rates' often have the highest team performance because they're brave enough to keep testing assumptions rather than playing it safe with proven approaches.

Curiosity conquers complacency: Jamie's breakthrough came from rediscovering the beginner's mind - attending different conferences, reading outside his field, and asking fresh voices for input.

Small experiments yield big insights: Quarterly empathy experiments in low-risk situations built Jamie's confidence to apply evolved approaches when stakes were high.

Evolution becomes contagious: When leaders model continuous learning, their teams naturally adopt similar growth mindsets, creating cultures of innovation and improvement.

The summit is a starting point: Every leadership success should be treated as a base camp for the next ascent, not a final destination to defend.

Your edge needs constant sharpening: The competitive advantage you've earned through success is only as valuable as your commitment to keep developing it through conscious evolution.

PART 3: TRANSCEND

> A society grows great when old men plant trees whose shade they know they shall never sit in.
> - Greek proverb[1]

Mastery isn't about being brilliant. It's about making brilliance contagious.

You've built the capability. You've transformed how you lead. Now comes the ultimate test: creating change that survives without you. This isn't about leaving a legacy. It's about starting a revolution that spreads beyond your control.

Navigate the conversations others avoid, turning conflict into breakthrough.

Lead through crisis when everything else fails and people need someone who can see clearly through chaos.

Revolutionise by embedding strategic empathy so deeply that it multiplies through others, creating cultures where understanding becomes automatic and empathy-driven leadership spreads like wildfire.

This is where individual excellence becomes systemic transformation; where your strategic empathy doesn't just improve your results but rewrites the rules for everyone who comes after you.

11: FROM TRAINWRECK TO MASTERY: WHY DIFFICULT CONVERSATIONS MAKE OR BREAK YOU

One of the most powerful examples of strategic empathy transformation I've witnessed comes from Kathy, a CEO in a fast-growing tech company. Her journey from avoiding difficult conversations to mastering them reveals principles that apply across any leadership context.

Kathy stared at her calendar and felt that familiar knot in her stomach. Three difficult conversations scheduled for this week: a performance review with her top performer who'd been struggling, a team conflict that was getting uglier by the day, and the devastating news about staff redundancies she had to deliver on Friday.

Six months ago, any one of these conversations would have kept her awake at night. She'd have spent hours rehearsing what to say, only to watch it all fall apart the moment emotions got involved. But something had changed. These conversations no longer felt like potential disasters waiting to happen. Kathy saw them as opportunities.

"How did you get so good at the hard stuff?" her colleague Mark asked after observing her handle a particularly tense team meeting. "You used to avoid conflict like the plague."

Kathy laughed. "I used to think difficult conversations were about saying the right words. Now I know they're about showing up the right way."

That transformation didn't happen overnight. It came through three specific breakdowns that forced Kathy to completely rethink how she approached the conversations that matter most.

Let me share her journey, because her failures and breakthroughs reveal everything you need to know about turning your most dreaded leadership moments into your greatest strengths.

Why your brain hijacks your best intentions

Kathy's first wake-up call came during what should have been a routine performance review with James, one of her talented team members. She'd prepared meticulously: notes, frameworks, even practiced her opening lines. She was going to be empathetic but clear, supportive and honest.

"So... how do you think this year went?" she began.

James shifted uncomfortably. "Uh... fine, I think? Pretty well?"

And there they were, stuck in that awkward dance where nobody says what they're really thinking. Kathy had pages of specific feedback, but she'd opened with a question that put James on the defensive before they'd even started.

The conversation that followed was painful for both of them. James became increasingly defensive as Kathy tried to work through her prepared points. She found herself getting frustrated, which made him shut down further. What should have been a development conversation became a defensive negotiation that helped no one.

"I don't understand," Kathy told me afterwards. "I said all the right things. I followed the process. But it felt like we were speaking different languages."

Here's what Kathy discovered that day: difficult conversations don't fail because we lack good intentions. They fail because we underestimate the emotional physics involved.

The moment everything goes sideways

Daniel Goleman calls it an 'amygdala hijack'[1]. It's that moment when your brain's alarm system takes over and rational thought goes out the window. It happens in milliseconds. Someone perceives a threat, and suddenly you're not dealing with thoughtful professionals anymore. You're dealing with nervous systems in survival mode.

In Kathy's conversation with James, her question triggered his brain's threat detection system. *Am I about to be criticised? Is my job at risk? Should I defend myself?* Meanwhile, his defensiveness triggered Kathy's own alarm bells: *He's not taking this seriously. He's making this difficult. I need to be more firm.*

Neither of them was wrong. They were just human. But understanding this changes everything about how you prepare for challenging conversations.

"I realised I'd been preparing for the conversation I wanted to have," Kathy reflected, "not the conversation his brain was actually going to experience."

Kathy's BRIDGE breakthrough

After that disaster with James, Kathy decided she needed a completely different approach. That's when she started applying the BRIDGE Framework not just as a communication tool, but as her emotional GPS for navigating difficult terrain.

Building awareness meant mapping the emotional landscape before stepping into it. Kathy started asking herself: What might James be worried about? What triggers does he have around feedback? What's my own emotional state, and how might it affect my delivery? How might I stop myself from becoming defensive if he pushes my buttons?

Recognising patterns came from studying her conversation failures. Kathy kept what she called a 'conversation journal'- not the content (that stayed confidential), but the emotional dynamics. What triggered defensiveness? When did people shut down? What approaches opened up dialogue?

The patterns that emerged surprised her. She discovered that her instinct to 'get to the point quickly' was actually creating more anxiety, not less. People needed time to adjust to difficult conversations, like walking into bright sunlight from a dark room.

Integrating empathy with strategy became Kathy's way of holding two truths simultaneously: I genuinely care about this person's success AND this conversation needs to produce specific outcomes. It wasn't empathy OR results. It was empathy FOR results.

Developing sustainable practices meant creating approaches that didn't depend on her having a perfect day. Because difficult conversations are exhausting, and if your method only works when you're at your best, it won't work when you need it most.

Generating lasting impact shifted Kathy's focus from 'surviving this conversation' to 'what do we build together because of this conversation'?

Evolving her approach meant treating every conversation that went differently than expected as data, not failure.

Six months later, Kathy had her next performance conversation with James.

Same person, same stakes, completely different outcome.

The performance review that changed everything

"James, I want to start by being clear about why we're here," Kathy began. "This isn't about judgment or evaluation in the traditional sense. It's about building on your strengths and identifying opportunities that excite you. My job isn't to tell you what's wrong. It's to help you see what's possible."

She watched James' shoulders relax slightly. Not completely as this was still a performance review, but enough to signal that his defensive systems weren't fully activated.

"I've been observing your work for months now," Kathy continued, "and I've seen things that impressed me and areas where I think you have enormous untapped potential. I'd like to share what I've noticed and get your thoughts on where you want to grow."

What followed was the most productive performance conversation Kathy had ever had.

James shared insights about his work that she'd never heard before.

He identified development areas that aligned perfectly with business needs.

They co-created a growth plan that energised both of them.

It didn't take long for James' performance to reach a new level. But more importantly, he'd started approaching challenges with curiosity instead of defensiveness. The conversation hadn't just improved his work. It had changed how he thought about feedback entirely.

"You helped me see that feedback wasn't an attack," James told Kathy months later. "It was an investment."

What Kathy learned about preparation

The difference wasn't just in Kathy's opening words. It was in how she'd prepared for the entire emotional journey.

Instead of just preparing her talking points, Kathy prepared for James' likely reactions. She anticipated his concerns about job security and had specific reassurances ready. She predicted his tendency to over-explain when nervous and planned to create space for that without getting derailed.

Most importantly, Kathy prepared herself emotionally. She did what she called 'emotional rehearsal', where she visualised the conversation going well, imagining James feeling supported rather than attacked, and connecting to her genuine desire to help him succeed.

"I stopped preparing for the conversation I wanted to give," Kathy explained, "and started preparing for the conversation he needed to receive."

The structure that actually works

Through trial and error, Kathy developed a reliable framework for performance conversations:

Foundation first (5 minutes): Set clear, positive intentions. "This conversation is about your growth and success."

Their voice first (15 minutes): "What are you most proud of? What's been challenging? Where do you see opportunities?" Listen for themes. Ask curious questions.

Your observations (15 minutes): Share specific examples that build on what they've said. Focus on patterns, not isolated incidents. Connect feedback to their stated goals.

Future focus (15 minutes): "Based on what we've discussed, here's what I'm excited about for you..." Co-create development plans that energise both of you.

Clear commitments (5 minutes): Document agreements from both sides. Set follow-up dates. End with encouragement.

"The magic wasn't in the structure," Kathy reflected. "It was in approaching the whole thing as a partnership instead of an evaluation."

When conflict became her secret weapon

Kathy's second breakthrough came when her team erupted into open conflict. Marcus from operations and Lisa from marketing had been sniping at each other for weeks. It started with a disagreement about timelines and escalated into personal attacks about competence and priorities.

Kathy's old approach would have been to smooth things over quickly by finding a compromise, redirecting their energy, and possibly separating them if necessary. She dreaded conflict and saw it as a sign of her leadership failure.

But something James had said during their transformed performance review stuck with her: "The best teams I've been on weren't afraid to disagree, they just knew how to disagree well."

So instead of avoiding the Marcus-Lisa situation, Kathy decided to lean into it.

Kathy called both of them into her office, took a deep breath, and said something that surprised them.

"I've been thinking about your disagreement, and I don't think we should solve it. I think we should understand it."

Marcus and Lisa looked confused. They'd expected her to referee their fight, not analyse it.

"Help me understand what's really at stake here," Kathy continued. "Not just the timeline question, but what this means to each of you."

What emerged over the next hour fascinated Kathy. Marcus wasn't just concerned about deadlines. He was also worried about sustainable processes and long-term quality. Lisa wasn't just pushing for speed. She was focused on market opportunities and competitive advantage.

Both were right. Both were serving the organisation's interests. They just had completely different perspectives on what the organisation needed most.

"Once we mapped out their underlying concerns," Kathy told me later, "the solution became obvious. We didn't need to choose between their approaches. We needed both perspectives informing every major decision."

What Kathy discovered about healthy conflict

The breakthrough with Marcus and Lisa taught Kathy something counterintuitive: conflict isn't the opposite of teamwork. Conflict is often the pathway to better teamwork.

When Marcus and Lisa stopped avoiding their disagreement and started exploring it, something remarkable happened. Their different perspectives combined to create solutions neither could have developed alone. Projects improved because they were stress-testing ideas before implementing them.

"I realised I'd been trying to create harmony," Kathy reflected, "when what my team actually needed was productive clash."

Teams that engage in healthy conflict consistently outperform teams that prioritise artificial harmony. Why? Because disagreement forces you to examine assumptions, consider alternatives, and test ideas under pressure [2].

But here's the crucial distinction Kathy learned: healthy conflict focuses on ideas and outcomes, not personalities and egos. The foundation is curiosity and assumes good intentions and explores different perspectives.

Unhealthy conflict attacks people, questions motives, and tries to win rather than learn. It turns colleagues into adversaries and discussions into battles where someone must lose for someone else to win.

Strategic empathy is what transforms potentially destructive disagreement into productive dialogue by helping you understand what's driving the other persons position before you challenge it.

Kathy's conflict navigation toolkit

Build awareness by mapping the emotional landscape before jumping into problem-solving. Kathy learned to ask: What is Marcus actually afraid will happen? What does Lisa need to feel heard? What values are being threatened on both sides? Think of it as checking the emotional temperature in the room.

Recognise patterns in how conflicts typically unfold, or how disagreements usually play out in your team. Kathy noticed that their most productive disagreements happened when people felt psychologically safe. Their most destructive conflicts happened when competence or motives were questioned or when people felt personally attacked.

Integrate empathy with strategy by holding space for emotions while staying focused on outcomes. "Conflict is emotional by nature," Kathy discovered. "The emotion signals that something important is at stake."

Develop sustainable practices by creating simple ground rules for how to disagree well within shared frameworks. Kathy's team developed what they called 'clean fighting rules', which were ways to challenge ideas without damaging relationships.

Generate lasting impact by using conflict as an opportunity to strengthen relationships. The best conflicts Kathy navigated didn't just solve immediate problems. They created deeper understanding and clearer expectations.

"The strangest thing happened," Kathy told me. "Once people saw that disagreement led to better solutions instead of damaged relationships, they started bringing up concerns earlier. We were solving problems before they became crises. The real magic happened when people stopped dreading conflict and started seeing it as a way to get closer to the truth together."

The news nobody wanted to hear

Kathy's third and most challenging test came with a phone call on a Tuesday morning. Budget cuts. Immediate restructuring. Two positions eliminated. And she had to tell her team by Friday.

This wasn't about performance issues or team dynamics. This was about people's livelihoods, their financial security, their faith that leadership would protect them. How do you tell dedicated employees that their positions are being eliminated despite their excellent work? How do you deliver life-changing news when you know the room will erupt with fear, anger, and disbelief?

Kathy's first instinct was to soften the blow, to cushion the message with explanations and apologies.

Her second instinct was to just rip off the band-aid and get it over with quickly. Both approaches felt wrong.

That's when she remembered the worst news she'd ever received as an employee.

The conversation that taught her everything

Years earlier, Kathy's previous boss had called her into his office and spent twenty minutes talking about budget pressures and difficult decisions before finally telling her that her program was being cut.

Those twenty minutes were torture. She knew something bad was coming, but she didn't know what. By the time he got to the actual news, she was so anxious she could barely process it. His attempt to soften the blow had made everything worse.

From that experience, Kathy learned that the kindest thing you can do when delivering tough news is to deliver it clearly and quickly, then spend your time on what comes next.

The conversation that restored her faith

When Kathy had to tell Jennifer that her position was being eliminated, she applied everything she'd learned about strategic empathy in high-stakes conversations.

"Jennifer, I have some very difficult news," Kathy began. "Due to budget cuts, we're eliminating your position. This decision has nothing to do with your performance or value to our team. It's purely financial, and I want to be completely clear about that."

Kathy watched Jennifer's face change as the reality hit. "I know this is shocking," she continued. "Take whatever time you need to process this."

What happened next surprised Kathy. Instead of anger or tears, Jennifer took a deep breath and said, "Thank you for being direct. I could tell something was wrong when you called this meeting. The not-knowing was worse than the knowing."

They spent the next thirty minutes talking about transition support, references, and how to communicate with the rest of the team. It wasn't an easy conversation, but it was respectful and honest.

Later, Jennifer told Kathy it was the most professional way she'd ever been let go. "You didn't make it about you or try to make me feel better," she said. "You just gave me the information I needed and then helped me figure out next steps."

Kathy's tough message framework

Through these challenging conversations, Kathy developed a reliable approach to delivering difficult news:

Lead with clarity, not cushioning: State the facts directly and immediately. Don't make people wait or guess.

Acknowledge the impact: "I know this is devastating news." Don't minimise or rush past their emotional response.

Focus on what you can control: Move quickly to support, resources, and next steps. Give people something concrete to work towards.

Create space for reaction: "What questions do you have? How can I help you right now?" Let them guide what they need in the moment.

Follow through consistently: Check in regularly during transitions. Keep your commitments about support and references.

"The paradox," Kathy reflected, "is that delivering bad news with strategic empathy can actually strengthen relationships. People remember not just what you told them, but how you made them feel when you told them."

The integration that matters most

Kathy's breakthrough wasn't mastering three separate skills, but discovering that performance reviews, conflict navigation, and tough message delivery are all variations on the same theme: how do you maintain human connection when emotions are high and stakes are personal?

The BRIDGE Framework works across all three because it addresses the fundamental challenge underlying every difficult conversation: how to honour both empathy and accountability, both feelings and facts, both the person in front of you and the larger purposes you serve.

Building your conversation confidence

The best way to develop confidence in difficult conversations isn't to practice on the most challenging ones. Kathy started with lower-stakes interactions where she could experiment with strategic empathy approaches without risking critical relationships.

She tried opening team meetings by acknowledging any tension she sensed in the room. She practiced giving specific, kind feedback on small issues before addressing major performance concerns. She experimented with asking curious questions instead of making assumptions about why people behaved the way they did.

Each small practice built her confidence for when the stakes were higher. She discovered that people responded positively when she led with genuine curiosity rather than judgment. The more she practiced staying present in uncomfortable moments, the less overwhelming they became. These smaller conversations taught her that vulnerability could be a strength, not a weakness, and that most people appreciated her directness when it came from a place of care.

"I stopped waiting for the perfect words," Kathy explained, "and started focusing on the perfect intentions. Once I trusted that my heart was in the right place, the words started flowing more naturally."

When strategic empathy just isn't enough

But let me be honest with you about something Kathy learned the hard way: not every difficult conversation has a happy ending. No matter how much strategic empathy you apply, no matter how perfectly you follow the BRIDGE framework, some conversations will still go badly.

Kathy discovered this during her most challenging conversation yet. It was with David, a long-tenured team member whose performance had been declining for months. She prepared meticulously, applied everything she'd learned, opened with empathy and clear intentions.

David's response? "This is complete bullshit. You have no idea what I've been dealing with, and frankly, I don't think you're qualified to judge my work."

The conversation spiralled from there. When Kathy tried to acknowledge his frustration, David interpreted it as condescension. Her attempts to understand his perspective were met with accusations that she was manipulating him. Each empathetic response seemed to fuel his anger rather than defuse it. The more she tried to steer the conversation toward problem-solving, the more he dug into attack mode. Despite Kathy's attempts to create space for his concerns, and redirect toward solutions, David became increasingly hostile.

"I did everything right," Kathy told me afterward. "I followed the framework perfectly. But it still went to hell."

Why some conversations fail despite your best efforts

Here's what Kathy learned from that painful experience: strategic empathy is powerful, but it's not magic. Sometimes conversations fail because:

The other person isn't ready. David was dealing with personal issues that made any feedback feel like an attack, regardless of how it was delivered. His defensive systems were so activated that empathy couldn't penetrate.

The relationship was already too damaged. Years of poor communication had created so much distrust that one conversation, no matter how skilful, couldn't repair it.

External pressures override everything. David was facing numerous personal concerns. In that moment, work feedback felt like the last straw, not an opportunity for growth.

Some people reject empathy. A small percentage of people interpret empathetic approaches as manipulation or weakness[5]. They prefer a direct confrontation approach.

Timing matters more than technique. Sometimes the conversation is right but the moment is wrong. David needed space to process his personal challenges before he could engage with professional feedback.

What to do when conversations go sideways

Kathy's breakthrough came not from avoiding future failures, but from learning how to recover from them:

Don't take it personally. David's reaction was about his circumstances, not Kathy's competence. The conversation failed, but that didn't make Kathy a failed leader.

Give it time. Three weeks after their disastrous meeting, David reached out to apologise and ask for another chance. Sometimes people need time to process before they can engage constructively.

Learn what you can, release what you can't. Kathy analysed what she might have done differently (maybe postponing the conversation when she saw David's stress level) but didn't torture herself over things beyond her control.

Maintain your standards anyway. Just because the conversation went badly didn't mean the performance issues disappeared. Kathy had to find other ways to address David's declining work while giving him space to stabilise personally.

Protect your own resilience. Failed conversations are emotionally draining. Kathy learned to debrief with trusted colleagues, practice self-care after difficult interactions, and remember that one bad conversation doesn't negate all the good ones.

But here's where Kathy discovered something that completely changed her understanding of leadership: the most important conversation isn't always the one you have with other people. It's the one you have with yourself afterward[6].

The choice that will define your career

Here's the choice every leader faces, and it's not the one you think: The question isn't whether you'll have difficult conversations.

They'll happen whether you participate or not.

The question is whether you'll be the leader creating breakthrough moments or the one being worked around while real leaders handle the conversations that matter.

Your team is already having difficult conversations about performance, conflict, and change. They're just not having them with you, especially if you've trained them that difficult conversations are dangerous, unwelcome, or pointless.

Meanwhile, somewhere in your organisation, there's a leader like Kathy. Someone who's worked out that difficult conversations aren't obstacles but the raw material of great leadership.

They're building the trust, driving the performance, and creating the culture that everyone else wishes they had.

The brutal truth? Every day you postpone mastering difficult conversations is another day that leader is pulling ahead of you. Every conflict you sidestep, every performance issue you delegate, every tough message you soften into meaninglessness, they are all evidence that you're not ready for the leadership roles you think you deserve.

But here's what gives me hope: Kathy wasn't born knowing how to have these conversations. She was terrified of them, failed at them, got feedback that they made her 'too soft'. She could have listened to that feedback and spent her career avoiding the very interactions that would define her legacy.

Instead, she chose to get dangerous.

This transformation, from conversation avoidance to conversation mastery, follows the same BRIDGE principles that

Jamie has been applying in his school leadership challenges. Whether you're managing a corporate team or leading an educational institution, the emotional dynamics remain consistent.

What kind of leader will you choose to become?

Will you be the one who builds a career on avoiding difficult conversations while wondering why breakthrough opportunities keep going to someone else?

Or will you be the one who realises that your next promotion, your next breakthrough, your next chance to create real change - and your ability to lead through any crisis - is waiting on the other side of the conversation you've been avoiding?

When crisis strikes, it's not your technical skills or strategic plans that will define your leadership. It's your willingness to have the conversations others won't. The conversation with the struggling team member everyone's given up on. The conversation with stakeholders when the project is failing. The conversation that acknowledges what's really happening when everyone else is pretending everything's fine.

Kathy made her choice three years ago. When her company faced its biggest crisis, she didn't hide behind emails or delegate the hard conversations to others. She stepped forward, spoke truth to power, and guided her team through the uncertainty with radical honesty and unwavering support.

Her team, her organisation, and her career will never be the same.

Crisis doesn't wait for you to be ready. But the leaders who emerge stronger are the ones who've already learned to have the conversations that matter.

Your most important conversation is waiting.

When will you be ready to have it?

Key Takeaways: From trainwreck to mastery

Difficult conversations fail because of emotional physics, not poor intentions: Daniel Goleman's 'amygdala hijack' explains why rational thought disappears when threat detection systems activate. Prepare for the conversation their brain will experience, not the one you want to have.

Three conversation killers strike instantly: Power triggers (feeling bulldozed), message gaps (confusion about meaning), and change shock (feeling unsettled by uncertainty). Spot these warning signs before they destroy dialogue.

The two-second choice determines everything: When resistance appears, you can either push through for compliance or pause and explore for commitment. Your response in these moments shapes whether you get collaboration or cooperation.

Kathy's transformation came through three breakdowns: Performance reviews that became defensive negotiations, team conflicts that revealed underlying values clashes, and delivering devastating news that taught her clarity beats cushioning. Each failure contained the seeds of mastery.

Strategic empathy isn't magic: Some conversations will fail despite perfect technique because people aren't ready, relationships are too damaged, external pressures overwhelm everything, or timing is simply wrong. Accept what you can't control while mastering what you can.

The BRIDGE Framework works across all difficult conversations: Whether performance reviews, conflict mediation, or tough message delivery, the same principles apply.

Recovery matters more than perfection: When conversations go sideways, don't take it personally, give people time, learn what you can while releasing what you can't, maintain standards and protect your resilience for the next challenge.

Your most important conversation is with yourself: The dialogue you have with yourself after difficult conversations, whether they succeed or fail, determines whether you become the leader who handles hard conversations or the one people work around when real leadership is needed.

12: FORGED IN FIRE: HOW CRISIS CAN MAKE A LEADER DANGEROUS

Kathy's mastery of difficult conversations was about to face its ultimate test. Having transformed her approach to performance reviews, conflict navigation, and delivering tough messages, she felt confident in her leadership abilities. But crisis has a way of exposing whether your skills are truly embedded or merely surface-level adaptations.

What happened next would reveal how the BRIDGE principles that work in individual challenging conversations scale to organisational upheaval, and whether strategic empathy can survive when everything you thought you knew about leadership gets tested in fire.

When everything falls apart, you discover what you're really made of…and who you're meant to become.

Kathy thought she had leadership worked out. She felt confident in her abilities.

Until one morning.

The email was casual enough: 'Emergency leadership meeting, 8am sharp.' Kathy assumed it was about the quarterly budget review running over schedule. By 8:30am, she was walking back to her office in complete shock. Their biggest client representing 40% of company revenue had terminated their contract effective immediately. Worse, they were publicly questioning the company's competence and threatening to damage relationships with other major clients.

"I just sat there staring at my computer screen," Kathy told me months later, "thinking that this can't be real. Everything I thought I knew about leadership was about to be tested in ways I never imagined."

What happened next would transform her from a competent manager into the kind of leader people turn to when their world is falling apart.

When normal rules don't apply

"The first thing that hit me," Kathy reflected, "was how different this felt from any difficult conversation I'd ever navigated. Those were challenging but contained. This was chaos spreading through the entire organisation."

Within an hour of the leadership meeting, rumours were flying. Marketing was panicking about campaign cancellations. Operations were fielding angry calls from suppliers worried about payment. Even the receptionist looked terrified.

This is where Kathy discovered the first crucial truth about crisis leadership: **building awareness** becomes absolutely critical, but it's not just about understanding facts. It's about mapping the emotional earthquake rippling through everyone around you.

Instead of hiding in her office crafting action plans, Kathy walked the floors to observe and listen. In marketing, she found Sarah stress-eating biscuits while frantically reworking campaigns. "Eight months of work just gone," Sarah groaned when she saw Kathy. "I don't even know if we'll have jobs next week."

Operations had Marcus fielding increasingly hostile supplier calls. "They're asking if we can still pay invoices," he told Kathy quietly. "Word's getting out that we're in trouble."

But in accounts, Lisa remained calm and methodical, already pulling together financial scenarios. "I've been through redundancies before," she said matter-of-factly. "The key is understanding exactly where we stand so we can make intelligent decisions."

"That's when I realised," Kathy told me, "that crises don't affect everyone the same way. Some people crumble, others panic, and some become incredibly focused. Understanding who was experiencing what became crucial for deciding out how to respond."

This awareness also helped Kathy **recognise patterns** from previous organisational crises she'd witnessed. Three years earlier, when another department had lost a major client, leadership had gone into hiding for days while rumours festered. By the time they emerged with a plan, the team was in disarray.

"I could see the same pattern starting," Kathy said, "with fear filling the information vacuum. I knew I had to act quickly."

The first 48 hours: when everything depends on what you do next

"Crisis leadership," Kathy discovered, "is less about having perfect answers and more about creating stability while you work out what the answers are."

The CEO had given department heads until Friday to present restructuring options. It was Tuesday morning. Kathy had three days to not only analyse the financial impact but to keep her team functional while everything felt like it was collapsing.

This is where **integrating empathy with strategy** became essential. Kathy couldn't separate the business decisions from the human impact because they were completely intertwined.

"If I approached this purely as a numbers exercise," she explained, "I'd miss crucial information about how to implement whatever plan I developed. But if I got lost in everyone's emotions, I'd never make the hard decisions that needed to be made."

She decided to be radically transparent with her team, but strategically so. Gathering everyone together Tuesday afternoon, she told them exactly what she knew, what she didn't know, and what she was going to find out.

"We've lost a major client, and that means changes are coming," she began. "I don't know yet what those changes will be, but I can tell you how I'm going to approach working that out. First, I'm going to understand exactly what our financial position is. Second, I'm going to explore every option for maintaining as many jobs as possible. Third, whatever changes we have to make, we're going to handle them with dignity and transparency."

What surprised Kathy was that her honesty seemed to reduce panic rather than increase it. "People told me later that the not-knowing had been worse than the knowing," she reflected. "Once they understood the process I was following, they could focus on their work instead of catastrophising about unknowns."

But Kathy also built her crisis response team from within existing relationships. She asked Marcus to help understand which projects could be paused, enlisted Sarah to think through client communications, and requested Lisa's help with financial modelling.

"I wasn't delegating decision-making," Kathy clarified, "but I was using their expertise and their emotional intelligence about the team to inform better decisions."

Leading when you don't have the answers

"The hardest part," Kathy told me, "wasn't making difficult decisions. It was leading confidently when I genuinely didn't know what was going to happen."

By Wednesday morning, the financial reality was stark: they needed to reduce costs by 30%. Traditional leadership wisdom might suggest projecting confidence and certainty. But Kathy had learned that authenticity builds trust faster than false confidence.

She gathered her team, outlining three possible scenarios and asking for their input. Instead of panic, her team started problem-solving with her. People volunteered information about career change considerations, skills overlap, and financial impacts that informed better decisions.

"I realised that **developing sustainable practices** in crisis means creating ways for people to contribute to solutions rather than just being victims of circumstances," Kathy explained. "When people can help solve problems, they feel less helpless."

But she also learned something crucial about managing her own emotional state. The constant pressure was exhausting in ways she hadn't anticipated. She found herself snapping at people, making decisions too quickly, then second-guessing everything.

"So I started what I called 'crisis rhythms,'" she said, "fifteen-minute walks between major decisions, daily check-ins with a trusted colleague, and acknowledging to myself that not having all the answers didn't make me a bad leader." Kathy had learned that stepping back to reset is crucial, and that effective leaders make peace with not knowing everything[1].

When emotions run high and stakes are higher

Thursday was when everything came to a head. Word had leaked about possible redundancies, and everyone was on edge. Kathy had to finalise her recommendations for Friday's leadership meeting while managing a team that was barely holding together.

This is where her experience with difficult conversations became invaluable and amplified. She wasn't just managing one challenging interaction; she was navigating multiple emotional minefields simultaneously.

David, who'd had performance issues for months, cornered her in the corridor with accusations.

Sarah was in tears in the break room, convinced she'd be let go just as she was planning her wedding.

Marcus was angry, pacing around muttering about loyalty and fairness.

"I realised that **strategic empathy under pressure** means understanding that people's reactions aren't really about you," Kathy reflected. "David's accusation was about his fear. Sarah's tears were about feeling powerless. Marcus's anger was about watching colleagues he cared about suffer."

Instead of getting defensive or trying to manage everyone's emotions, she addressed the underlying concerns directly through individual meetings. Not to deliver decisions but to understand what they were most worried about and what information would help them feel more secure.

What she discovered was that different people needed different things. Some needed more information about the process. Others needed reassurance about their value to the team. A few just needed acknowledgements that the situation was genuinely difficult. Effective leaders recognise that each team member values different forms of communication, ranging from information to emotional support, and adapt accordingly[2].

But here's where Kathy's crisis leadership hit its first major hurdle.

When strategic empathy isn't enough

Despite all her careful preparation and empathetic approach, not everyone responded well. David became increasingly hostile throughout the week, spreading negativity among team members and openly questioning Kathy's competence. Her attempts to address his concerns directly only seemed to fuel his anger.

By Thursday evening, David's behaviour was affecting team morale. People were avoiding him, and his conspiracy theories about the redundancy process were creating additional anxiety. Sarah, already emotional about the uncertainty, became even more upset after David suggested the decisions had already been made.

"The consultation process is just for show," he told anyone who would listen. "They've already decided who's going."

Kathy faced a difficult realisation: sometimes strategic empathy alone isn't sufficient. Some people's emotional responses can become toxic to the broader team, and continuing to accommodate destructive behaviour can undermine your ability to lead others through crisis[3].

She made the tough decision to have a final, direct conversation with David. "David, I understand you're frightened about your future here," she began, "but your current approach is damaging to colleagues who are already struggling. I need you to either engage constructively with this process or step back from it entirely."

David's response was to escalate further and threaten to speak to senior leadership about her unfair treatment.

The situation became a significant distraction during the most critical phase of crisis planning.

"This taught me a hard lesson about crisis leadership," Kathy told me. "You cannot save everyone, and attempting to do so can compromise your ability to help those who are genuinely willing to work through difficult circumstances constructively."

When plans meet reality

Friday morning arrived, and Kathy presented her restructuring plan to the leadership team. Her final recommendation was nuanced: two voluntary redundancies with enhanced packages, two role consolidations, and two difficult decisions about positions that genuinely couldn't be sustained.

The plan was approved, but implementation got messy. The person she'd hoped would leave voluntarily declined, forcing a difficult termination conversation. A role consolidation that looked logical on paper created friction between two team members with personality conflicts she'd missed. Worst of all, David escalated to HR, creating a formal grievance that distracted from the broader transition. "I thought I'd planned for everything," Kathy reflected, "but implementation is always messier than planning. People aren't spreadsheet entries, they're complex individuals with their own fears, aspirations, and relationships." It's vital to keep this in mind when implementing these plans.

The restructuring was completed within six weeks, but it wasn't the smooth transition Kathy had envisioned. Two key relationships were damaged.

"I learned that **generating lasting impact** from crisis doesn't mean achieving perfect outcomes," Kathy said. "Sometimes it means achieving the best possible outcomes under impossible circumstances while accepting that some relationships and situations cannot be salvaged." The measure of transcendent leadership isn't whether you can save everything, but whether you can maintain your integrity and empathy even in impossible situations.

What crisis teaches you about yourself

Six months later, Kathy's restructured team was working effectively, but the path had been far from smooth.

The people who remained had developed new skills and deeper collaboration, but it had taken months to rebuild trust after the disruption.

David had ultimately been performance-managed out of the organisation within two months of the restructuring, but not before creating ongoing tension and requiring significant management time that could have been better spent supporting other team members.

"Looking back," Kathy told me, "I realised that crisis hadn't taught me completely new leadership skills. It had forced me to apply everything I'd learned about difficult conversations at much higher intensity and broader scale. The BRIDGE framework that had transformed my approach to individual challenging conversations became my compass through organisational crisis."

But the biggest discovery was about her own capacity and limitations. "I'd always thought of myself as someone who avoided conflict and uncertainty," she said. "Crisis showed me I could not only handle it, but could help others handle it too. It also taught me that leadership sometimes means making decisions that some people will never forgive you for."

Crisis made Kathy dangerous in the best possible way. "It made me dangerous to problems that seemed unsolvable," she laughed. "Dangerous to cultures that avoided difficult truths, and dangerous to the idea that you must choose between caring about people and getting results."

The conversation that changed everything wasn't one she had with someone else. It was the conversation she had with herself about what kind of leader she wanted to become when everything was falling apart. And most importantly, what kind of leader she could realistically be when perfect solutions don't exist[5].

That confidence would be tested again just three months later, though not another crisis, but through the quiet complexity of leading people she could barely see.

Key Takeaways: How crisis forges dangerous leaders

Crisis amplifies rather than replaces existing leadership capabilities: The difficult conversation skills Kathy had developed became the foundation for crisis leadership. Strategic empathy proved even more powerful when applied across organisational upheaval but required adaptation to new scales.

Building awareness during crisis means mapping emotional earthquakes: Understanding how crisis affects different people in different ways provides crucial intelligence for decision-making.

Transparency reduces panic more than false reassurance: Sharing what you know, what you don't know, and how you're finding out creates stability in uncertainty. People's fear of the unknown is often worse than their fear of difficult realities.

Strategic empathy has limits and cannot fix everyone: Not every person will respond constructively to empathetic leadership during crisis. Some individuals' emotional responses become toxic to the broader team, requiring difficult decisions about boundaries and acceptable behaviour.

Perfect outcomes are impossible, but integrity in process matters: Crisis leadership rarely produces ideal results for everyone involved. Success means achieving the best possible outcomes under impossible circumstances while maintaining dignity and transparency at all times.

Sustainable practices prevent leader burnout when teams need you most: Crisis leadership requires emotional resilience that only comes from deliberate self-care and structured approaches. Regular rhythms and support systems ensure effectiveness throughout extended pressure.

Implementation is always messier than planning: Even well-designed crisis responses encounter unexpected complications.

Crisis reveals leadership capacity while teaching realistic limitations: Challenging situations expose true capabilities while also demonstrate that no leadership approach, however empathetic, can satisfy everyone or prevent all negative outcomes.

13: LEADING ACROSS DISTANCES: THE NEW FRONTIER FOR REMOTE LEADERSHIP

When crisis goes digital

Over the course of eighteen months, Kathy had transformed from avoiding difficult conversations to navigating organisational crisis. Six months after successfully leading her team through the major client loss and restructuring, she faced an unexpected new challenge. Her company announced a permanent shift to hybrid working, which involved three days remote, two in the office. Suddenly, the strategic empathy skills that had served her so well in face-to-face crisis situations needed translating to a digital world. Although the crisis had taught Kathy that she thrived under pressure and could guide others through uncertainty, this new phase of hybrid work posed different challenges that required different applications of strategic empathy.

"How do you read the room when there is no room?" she asked during one of our coaching sessions. It's a question that captures the fundamental challenge facing many leaders today.

The transition from managing difficult conversations in person to leading across distances isn't just a tactical shift but a complete reimagining of how strategic empathy works. Those subtle facial expressions that helped Kathy gauge her team's stress levels during the crisis? Gone. The ability to pull someone aside for a quiet word after a heated meeting? Replaced by awkward breakout rooms and delayed responses to messages.

Yet here's what Kathy discovered over the following months: strategic empathy doesn't diminish across digital distances, it intensifies. When physical presence disappears, intentional emotional connection becomes your most powerful leadership tool.

The invisible leadership challenge

The statistics tell a sobering story. Most professionals now prefer hybrid arrangements, yet the majority of organisations lack proper strategies for this reality[1]. Leaders who master remote leadership see dramatically higher productivity and retention rates[2]. This isn't about adapting to temporary circumstances; it's about seizing a permanent competitive advantage.

But here's the paradox: whilst technology connects us globally, it often leaves us feeling more isolated than ever. Kathy's leaner but stronger team with Sarah in marketing, Lisa in accounts, and two new hires who'd joined post-restructuring, began describing themselves as 'the city crew' rather than simply 'us'. The very tool meant to unite was creating division.

Strategic empathy offers the solution. It transforms virtual leadership from a communication challenge into a connection opportunity. The principles remain unchanged. It's the application that evolves[3].

Digital presence: beyond the screen

When Kathy first attempted to replicate her in-person leadership style online, disaster struck. Her carefully crafted email about project deadlines triggered a team-wide panic. What she'd intended as encouragement, her team read as criticism.

The message that would have worked perfectly when addressing everyone in the room, delivered with a smile and supportive tone, became a source of anxiety in text form.

The science explains why digital miscommunication happens so frequently. Our brains have evolved to read emotions through facial expressions, body language, and vocal tone. Video calls provide some of these cues, but text messages offer virtually none. This is why that innocent email can explode into workplace drama. Our brains fill the emotional gaps with assumptions, often negative ones[4].

Successful remote leaders like Kathy learn that digital presence isn't about writing better emails; it's about choosing better channels[5]. When tensions rise, she picks up the phone. For nuanced conversations, she opts for video calls. Voice messages convey the warmth that text simply cannot capture.

But the deeper insight proved more powerful: effective remote leaders communicate more frequently than their office counterparts, not through endless meetings, but through intentional micro-connections[6]. Kathy began sending two-minute voice notes celebrating successes, offered quick check-ins after difficult client calls, and shared brief personal updates. This approach echoed what Jamie, a school principal I was also mentoring, had discovered in education: "When you can't see people regularly, you have to be more intentional about celebrating the small wins. Those voice messages became my way of walking the corridors digitally."

Building trust without coffee chats

Trust, that invisible currency of leadership, becomes both more challenging and more critical in remote settings[7]. During the supply chain crisis, Kathy had built trust through visible calm and consistent presence. But how do you demonstrate reliability when your team can't see you?

The answer surprised her. Virtual trust requires radical transparency. When Kathy shifted from delivering polished, scripted communications to sharing her actual thought processes, including uncertainties and mistakes, something happened.

Problems surfaced faster. Solutions emerged collaboratively.

This wasn't unique to Kathy's experience. Across the leaders I coached, the same pattern emerged. Jamie in education had found that strategic empathy meant being honest about not having all the answers - abandoning formal communications for authentic acknowledgment of shared uncertainty.

This transparency imperative has a crucial counterpart: the death of surveillance-based management. Traditional oversight becomes impossible and counterproductive in remote settings[8]. Kathy learned to focus obsessively on outcomes whilst giving her team complete autonomy over methods.

Research confirms what Kathy discovered: high-trust teams outperform low-trust teams substantially whilst appearing to 'work' less[9]. They take longer breaks, have more casual conversations, yet deliver superior results. Trust eliminates the hidden tax of defensive documentation, carefully worded emails, and performative busyness that plagues suspicious environments.

BRIDGE in the digital age

Strategic empathy's BRIDGE framework adapts beautifully to remote leadership, though each element requires digital translation:

Build awareness becomes about reading digital signals. Kathy learned to track response times, monitor engagement in virtual meetings, and notice who contributed to online discussions. When team member Sarah's usual enthusiastic participation dropped to silence, Kathy reached out privately, discovering personal challenges that were affecting work.

Recognise patterns shifts to understanding communication preferences across your team. Some people excel in video calls but struggle with written feedback. Others prefer asynchronous discussions over real-time meetings. Kathy mapped these preferences, then adapted her approach accordingly.

Integrate empathy with strategy means balancing human connection with performance accountability. Kathy began combining personal check-ins with goal discussions, creating space for both relationship and results.

Develop sustainable practices becomes establishing digital rituals that create consistency across distance. Kathy's team adopted Monday voice message updates and Friday celebration calls. These were simple practices that maintained connection without overwhelming calendars.

Generate lasting impact and Evolve and adapt focus on building systems that work regardless of location. When team members could participate equally whether at home or in office, the artificial divide between remote and present disappeared.

The hybrid challenge: avoiding the two-tier system

Perhaps nowhere is strategic empathy more crucial than in hybrid teams. Kathy discovered that mixing in-person and remote participants often creates a caste system - office workers get the inside track whilst remote colleagues become second-class citizens[10].

Her solution? The 'one team, one experience' principle. When anyone joins remotely, everyone operates as if remote. Meetings happen on individual screens even for co-located staff. Decisions await input from all team members. Important discussions get documented for transparency.

The office-based team members initially protested, but within weeks, collaboration improved and the us-versus-them mentality evaporated. This approach works because it eliminates proximity bias, our unconscious tendency to favour people we see physically[11].

Making it sustainable

True remote leadership excellence isn't about perfecting video call techniques or mastering collaboration software. It's about recognising that distance amplifies the need for intentional human connection. Every interaction becomes an opportunity to demonstrate strategic empathy[12]. When you can't read body language through a screen or sense the energy in the room, you must become more deliberate about understanding what people are experiencing.

The casual conversations that once happened naturally by the coffee machine must now be consciously created. What was once spontaneous feedback now requires structured check-ins, and the emotional intelligence that developed organically in face-to-face environments must be cultivated with purpose and precision in digital spaces.

Kathy's transformation culminated in a realisation that surprised her: "I thought remote work would make leadership more technical. Instead, it made it more human. When you can't rely on physical presence, you have to rely on emotional intelligence."

Her team's engagement scores now exceed pre-remote levels. Productivity has increased measurably. Most tellingly, when the company offered a return to full-time office working, Kathy's team unanimously chose to maintain their hybrid model, not for convenience, but because they'd discovered a more empathetic way of working together.

The universal application

The principles that enable thriving distributed teams extend far beyond formal reporting relationships. Strategic empathy skills that bridge digital divides work equally well when influencing across organisational hierarchies, managing stakeholder relationships, or leading change initiatives[13].

Jamie's experience confirms this insight: "Remote leadership forced me to become a better leader overall. The skills I developed connecting across distance made me more effective in every leadership situation."

Kathy's transformation reveals something profound: the intentional connection required for effective remote leadership makes all leadership more powerful. When you learn to create authentic relationships across digital distances, face-to-face interactions become richer. When you master reading emotional signals through screens and messages, you become more attuned to subtle cues in every context.

Beyond individual mastery

As Kathy watched her approach influence other managers, as she saw her team members carry these principles into their own leadership opportunities, as the ripple effects spread beyond her direct control, she began to grapple with leadership's ultimate frontier.

The future belongs to leaders who don't just connect authentically across distances; they create systems that sustain authentic connection long after they've moved on. Because true leadership in our interconnected world isn't measured by what you achieve while you're present. It's defined by what continues to flourish in your absence[14].

The question isn't whether you can lead through screens and spreadsheets. It's whether you can build something that thrives when the screen goes dark and someone else takes your place. It's whether your strategic empathy becomes so embedded in others that your impact grows stronger, not weaker, when you're no longer in the room.

This is where individual excellence transforms into something far more powerful: legacy that transcends any single leader, any single crisis, any single distance that needs to be bridged.

Key Takeaways: Strategic empathy bridges any distance

Distance amplifies rather than diminishes the need for strategic empathy: When physical presence disappears, emotional connection becomes your most powerful leadership tool. The micro-connections and intentional touchpoints that replace casual office interactions require more deliberate empathy, not less.

Communication channel selection becomes a strategic empathy decision: Choose your medium based on emotional complexity - phone calls for tension, video for nuance, voice messages for warmth. Digital miscommunication happens when we ignore the human need for emotional context that different channels provide.

Virtual trust demands radical transparency over polished performance: Sharing your thought processes, uncertainties, and mistakes creates psychological safety across digital distances. High-trust remote teams outperform surveillance-based management because trust eliminates the hidden tax of defensive behaviours.

The 'One Team, One Experience' principle eliminates proximity bias: When anyone joins remotely, everyone operates as if remote to ensure equal participation. This approach prevents the two-tier system that naturally develops when physical presence creates unconscious advantages.

Digital rituals replace spontaneous office connections: Consistent touchpoints like Monday voice messages and Friday celebrations maintain team connection without overwhelming calendars. These structured practices become more important than formal meetings for building relationships across distance.

Remote leadership mastery creates transcendent impact: The intentional connection required for digital leadership enhances every leadership interaction. But the ultimate test isn't personal competence, it's whether your strategic empathy becomes so embedded in others that it survives and spreads beyond your direct influence.

14: BEYOND THE BRIDGE: YOUR STRATEGIC EMPATHY REVOLUTION

> The ultimate test of leadership isn't what you achieve while you're present, but what continues to flourish in your absence.
>
> - (Anonymous, n.d.)[1].

When individual mastery meets systemic transformation

Sometimes the answer to a question that's haunted you arrives not as an epiphany, but as a quiet recognition of what was already taking shape around you. And that question was: "What happens when I'm no longer here to model this?"

Jamie's question from many months earlier had stayed with me, echoing through every conversation about leadership development. But recently, I experienced something that showed me the true power of strategic empathy's ripple effect in ways I never could have imagined.

To understand this, I need to go back to what happened in that government office years ago.

The moment that revealed everything

The revelation about transcendent leadership came to me through watching profound insights die in what I see as 'institutional indifference'.

I was sitting in that sterile government office, carrying knowledge I'd never wanted to possess. My friend's suicide had taught me truths about leadership isolation that no training manual could capture. I had solutions born from grief, understanding forged through loss, and an unshakeable conviction that other leaders shouldn't face what he'd endured alone.

But the institution saw my hard-won wisdom as inconvenient disruption.

"We need to ensure alignment with existing frameworks," came the response from bureaucrats whose closest encounter with leadership pressure was reading about it in reports. They used procedural authority to silence what experience had taught me.

What could have saved lives became policy considerations for future review.

Meanwhile, the leaders I was trying to help remained trapped in the same isolation that had consumed my friend.

That afternoon, surrounded by people who confused position with wisdom, I understood something crucial: even the most profound insights become powerless when systems are designed to resist them. I realised my entire approach to leadership had been incomplete. I'd been trying to inject wisdom into structures that couldn't receive it.

The problem wasn't that people didn't understand good leadership principles. The issue was that the organisational machinery itself was programmed to crush exactly the behaviours we claimed to value. We said we wanted empathetic leaders, then promoted the people who made the fastest decisions without consulting anyone. We talked about collaboration, then structured meetings where speaking up meant derailing the agenda. We preached teamwork, then designed performance reviews that pitted colleagues against each other for limited rewards. We created environments hostile to what we really wanted to create.

What I see now that I couldn't see then

Today, as I write these words, something profound has shifted in the leadership landscape. It's something that connects directly to the mastery you've witnessed in leaders like Kathy and Jamie, something that might have saved my friend's life if it had existed then.

Jamie, the principal you've journeyed with throughout this book, faced his own impossible moment last month. But now, in his regional leadership role, the challenge came from one of the schools under his guidance.

A teacher in crisis, just like my friend had been. But this time, the story unfolded differently.

Instead of institutional barriers blocking human understanding, the principal Jamie had been mentoring led a school where emotional intelligence was valued as highly as operational efficiency. Where difficult conversations happened before crises erupted. Where strategic empathy wasn't a nice-to-have soft skill but the backbone of how decisions got made.

When Lina, a talented teacher struggling with depression and overwhelming pressure, finally found the courage to ask for help, she didn't meet bureaucratic walls. She met a principal who had learned from Jamie to see what others miss, who understood that her struggle wasn't a performance management issue but a human being in pain who needed support, not judgment.

The conversation that principal had with Lina - applying every principle of the BRIDGE framework Jamie had shared - didn't just save her career. It quite possibly saved her life.

And here's what stops me in my tracks. That principal learned these skills from Jamie. But Jamie learned them from me. And I learned them from the failure to save my friend. The strategic empathy capabilities that enabled connection across distances, whether physical, emotional, or hierarchical, had become so embedded in the leadership culture that they operated automatically when crisis struck.

Lina is alive and thriving today because individual mastery had transformed into something far more powerful: systemic capability that survived and thrived independent of any single leader's presence.

That's the power of strategic empathy's ripple effect. That's what transcendence actually looks like.

The revolution hiding in plain sight

What you've learned throughout this book isn't just another leadership methodology. You've become part of a quiet revolution that's transforming how human beings relate to each other in positions of power.

Think about the leaders whose stories we've followed:

Jamie didn't just transform his school. Now overseeing 300 schools across the region, he facilitates strategic empathy throughout a large educational system. His approach spreads through the principals he mentors, the policies he influences, and the culture he shapes at scale. The teachers he developed are leading their own schools with empathy-driven approaches, while students who experienced his leadership carry those expectations forward, demanding nothing less than leaders who genuinely understand them. One principal's transformation has become systemic change touching thousands of educators and tens of thousands of young lives.

Kathy didn't just navigate her crisis successfully. Her approach became a case study that influenced how her entire organisation handles difficult transitions. The team members she supported through that traumatic restructuring now model the same integration of empathy and strategy in their own leadership roles. The ripples continue spreading.

The healthcare director who revolutionised patient care protocols. The tech manager who transformed meeting culture. The government official who bridged departmental silos. Each one started with personal transformation but created systemic change that outlasts their tenure.

This is what I missed all those years ago in that sterile government office. I was trying to inject wisdom into a system designed to resist it. What I should have been doing was what you're doing now: becoming the kind of leader who creates systems that welcome wisdom.

The choice that defines your legacy

But here's where your real journey begins. Everything you've learned, every framework you've mastered, every difficult conversation you've navigated successfully, they all lead to this moment of choice.

You can use strategic empathy to become a better leader. That's valuable.

Or you can use strategic empathy to become an agent of transformation. That's transcendent.

The difference isn't subtle. Better leaders optimise existing systems. Agents of transformation create new possibilities that didn't exist before.

Better leaders apply the BRIDGE framework to their own interactions and see improved results.

Agents of transformation embed strategic empathy so deeply into organisational DNA that it becomes how business gets done, even when they're not in the room.

Better leaders have great one-on-one relationships and productive team meetings.

Agents of transformation create cultures where strategic empathy spreads virally, where people naturally begin treating each other with the same understanding they've experienced.

Better leaders solve today's problems more effectively.

Agents of transformation prevent tomorrow's crises by addressing the human dynamics that create them.

What the world looks like when empathy wins

When empathy wins, the world transforms in ways that feel almost magical. Picture walking into an organisation where strategic empathy isn't some rare exception, it's simply how things are done.

Conversations that used to drain energy now happen naturally and early.

People trust they'll be heard with understanding rather than judgment, so they speak up before small issues become big problems.

Innovation flourishes because psychological safety makes creative risk-taking feel possible rather than dangerous.

Conflict resolves constructively as people assume good intentions and explore different perspectives rather than defending positions like territory.

Change initiatives succeed because leaders understand what drives resistance and address underlying concerns rather than pushing through with authority.

Performance management becomes about development and partnership, with feedback offered through genuine care for growth rather than compliance.

Crisis situations bring out collective wisdom from every level because people know their insights will be valued regardless of hierarchy.

This isn't utopian fantasy. It's what happens when enough leaders choose strategic empathy over positional authority.

I've seen it. I've helped create it. And once you experience it, you can never go back to the old way of leading.

The conversation that changes everything

But transformation doesn't happen in the abstract. It happens in specific moments, in actual conversations, with real people facing genuine challenges.

Right now, somewhere in your sphere of influence, there's someone struggling in silence. Someone whose wisdom is being dismissed because they lack authority. Someone whose innovative ideas are dying in bureaucratic approval processes. Someone facing the crushing isolation of leadership responsibility without adequate support.

The strategic empathy revolution begins with your willingness to have the conversation others are avoiding.

Maybe it's the performance conversation you've been postponing because you're dreading the conflict.

The team member whose potential you see but whose confidence has been shattered by previous leaders.

The organisational dysfunction everyone complains about privately, but no one addresses publicly.

The policy that made sense on paper but creates human suffering in practice.

The colleague who's been marginalised because their communication style doesn't fit cultural norms.

The innovation that's been killed by risk-averse bureaucracy.

Your strategic empathy skills, every component of the BRIDGE framework you've mastered, have prepared you for this moment.

Beyond personal mastery: the multiplication effect

Here's what separates good leaders from transcendent ones: the willingness to make your transformation contagious.

When you consistently model strategic empathy, people begin mirroring your approach without conscious effort. Your emotional regulation becomes their emotional regulation. Your curiosity about others' perspectives becomes their default stance. Your integration of empathy with strategy becomes their problem-solving methodology.

Jamie discovered this when his assistant principal began naturally applying integration principles during a parent conflict, not because she'd been trained but because she'd absorbed the approach through observation.

Kathy realised it when team members started acknowledging each other's concerns before proposing solutions, not because it was policy but because it had become cultural norm.

This multiplication effect is how individual transformation becomes organisational revolution. It's how your leadership creates change that outlasts your presence.

The ultimate test

The ultimate test of your strategic empathy mastery isn't whether you can navigate difficult conversations or lead through crisis. It's whether you can create conditions where others develop these capabilities naturally.

When people leave your team, do they carry your empathetic leadership approach to their next role?

When you're not in the room, do decisions still get made with the same integration of understanding and strategy?

When crisis strikes your organisation, do people instinctively respond with curiosity rather than defensiveness because that's the culture you've helped create?

This is transcendence. Not just becoming better yourself but becoming the catalyst for others' transformation.

Your invitation to transcendence

The strategic empathy revolution doesn't need your permission to continue. It's already happening in organisations around the world as leaders discover that understanding outperforms authority, that influence trumps control, that human connection drives sustainable results.

But it needs your participation to accelerate.

Every time you choose curiosity over judgment, you make that choice more available to others.

Every time you integrate empathy with strategy, you demonstrate that false choice between caring or results.

Every time you create psychological safety for difficult conversations, you prove that authenticity strengthens rather than weakens organisational effectiveness.

Every time you develop another leader's strategic empathy capabilities, you multiply your impact beyond anything you could achieve alone.

The conversation that's waiting for you

So, here's my final challenge to you: what's the one conversation you've been avoiding? The one that feels too difficult, too risky, too uncertain? The one where your old leadership instincts tell you to use authority or wait for someone else to handle it?

That conversation is your portal to transcendence.

Everything you've learned throughout this book, every framework, every insight, every story of transformation, has prepared you for this moment. The BRIDGE framework you've mastered isn't just a communication tool. It's your compass for navigating the unknown territory where real leadership happens.

The person on the other side of that conversation isn't an obstacle to overcome or a problem to solve. They're a human being with their own wisdom, fears, hopes, and potential. They're waiting for a leader who sees them not as a position on an organisational chart but as a complete person deserving of understanding.

They're waiting for someone exactly like the leader you're becoming.

The legacy that writes itself

When you step into that conversation with strategic empathy as your guide, you're not just solving an immediate problem. You're modelling a different way of being in relationship with power. You're demonstrating that authority and empathy aren't opposites but partners. You're proving that the most strategic thing any leader can do is genuinely understand the people they serve.

And that person will remember. Not just what you decided or how you solved their problem, but how you made them feel when they were vulnerable. How you listened when they shared their truth. How you honoured their humanity while advancing organisational purposes.

They'll carry that experience with them. They'll expect it from future leaders. They'll provide it to others when they assume leadership roles.

The conversation you have today creates the leadership culture of tomorrow.

Beyond the bridge

The bridge that gives this framework its name isn't just about connecting empathy with strategy, though it does that. It isn't just about spanning the gap between understanding and action, though it accomplishes that too.

The BRIDGE you've built through this journey connects who you were as a leader with who you're capable of becoming. It spans the chasm between authority-based management and influence-driven leadership. It carries you from personal effectiveness to transcendent impact.

But most importantly, it creates a pathway for others to follow.

The bridge you've built doesn't disappear when you cross it. It remains, creating safe passage for every leader who comes after you. Every person you develop, every culture you transform, every conversation you revolutionise becomes part of the infrastructure that makes strategic empathy more accessible to the next generation of leaders.

The revolution continues

Somewhere right now, a leader is discovering that their team performs better when they feel genuinely understood.

Another is realising that their most challenging employee just needed someone to acknowledge their concerns before addressing their behaviour.

A third is learning that strategic empathy doesn't make them weak but makes them dangerous to the status quo.

They don't know they're part of a revolution. They just know something has shifted in how they think about leadership. Something that makes their work more effective and more meaningful simultaneously.

They're following a bridge you helped build.

My friend deserved better than a system that valued process over people. Your team deserves better than leadership that prioritises position over potential. The people you lead, the organisations you influence, the problems you're positioned to solve, they all deserve leaders who understand that the most strategic thing you can do is genuinely care about human beings.

You've learned to be that leader. Now the question is: what will you do with that power?

The strategic empathy revolution isn't waiting for permission. It's waiting for you.

Welcome to transcendence. Welcome to the other side of the bridge.

The conversation that changes everything is yours to have.

When will you be ready to have it?

NOTES

Introduction

1. Farh, J.-L., & Cheng, B.-S. (2000). A cultural analysis of paternalistic and authoritarian leadership. In J. T. Li, A. S. Tsui, & E. Weldon (Eds.), Management and organizations in the Chinese context (pp. 84–127). Palgrave Macmillan.
2. Gallup, Inc. (2024). State of the global workplace: 2024 report. Gallup Press. https://www.gallup.com/workplace/349484/state-of-the-global-workplace.aspx
3. Goleman, D. (2013). The focused leader. Harvard Business Review, 91(12), 50–60.
4. Sapolsky, R. M. (2015). Behave: The biology of humans at our best and worst. Penguin Press.
5. Kock, H., & Shepherd, G. J. (2022). Strategic empathy: How managers can effectively use empathy as a "hard" strategic capability. Business Horizons, 65(5), 559–569. https://doi.org/10.1016/j.bushor.2022.02.008

Part 1

1. Elliot, J. (2011). The Steve Jobs way: iLeadership for a new generation. Vanguard Press.

Chapter 1

1. Blanchard, K. H. (1985). Leadership and the one minute manager: Increasing effectiveness through situational leadership. William Morrow.
2. Finerman, W. (Producer), & Frankel, D. (Director). (2006). The devil wears Prada [Film]. 20th Century Fox.
3. Catmull, E. (2008). How Pixar fosters collective creativity. Harvard Business Review, 86(9), 64–72.

4. Singer, T., & Klimecki, O. M. (2014). Empathy and compassion. Current Biology, 24(18), R875–R878. https://doi.org/10.1016/j.cub.2014.06.054
5. Rock, D., & Schwartz, J. (2006). The neuroscience of leadership. Strategy+Business, 43, 1–10.
6. Goleman, D., & Boyatzis, R. (2008). Social intelligence and the biology of leadership. Harvard Business Review, 86(9), 74–81.
7. Rock, D. (2008). SCARF: A brain-based model for collaborating with and influencing others. NeuroLeadership Journal, 1, 44–52.

Chapter 2

1. Stewart, D. (2017). Carlos Ghosn: Power, leadership and the Nissan turnaround. In H. Miyoshi & M. A. Wada (Eds.), Alliance strategy and corporate governance: Renault, Nissan, and Daimler (pp. 71–93). Palgrave Macmillan. https://doi.org/10.1057/978-1-137-57426-1_5
2. Tabuchi, H., & Rich, M. (2018, November 22). Nissan board removes Carlos Ghosn as chairman after his arrest. The New York Times. https://www.nytimes.com/2018/11/22/business/nissan-carlos-ghosn-dismissal.html
3. Microsoft case study [Data file]. (2025). Microsoft toxic workplace case study.
4. Nadella, S., & Shaw, G. (2017). Hit refresh: The quest to rediscover Microsoft's soul and imagine a better future for everyone. Harper Business.
5. Gallo, A. (2017, November). How Microsoft became a 'growth mindset' company. Harvard Business Review. https://hbr.org/2017/11/how-microsoft-became-a-growth-mindset-company
6. Rock, D. (2008). SCARF: A brain-based model for collaborating with and influencing others. NeuroLeadership Journal, 1, 44–52.
7. Lieberman, M. D., & Eisenberger, N. I. (2009). Pains and pleasures of social life. Science, 323(5916), 890–891. https://doi.org/10.1126/science.1170008

8. Fang, F., Han, Z., Wang, X., & Chen, Y. (2018). A dual route model of empathy: A neurobiological perspective. Frontiers in Psychology, 9, Article 2212. https://doi.org/10.3389/fpsyg.2018.02212
9. Rock, D. (2008). SCARF: A brain-based model for collaborating with and influencing others. NeuroLeadership Journal, 1, 44–52.
10. Microsoft. (2016, June 13). Microsoft to acquire LinkedIn. Microsoft News. https://news.microsoft.com/source/2016/06/13/microsoft-to-acquire-linkedin/
11. Goleman, D. (2006). Social intelligence: The new science of human relationships. Bantam Books.
12. Peoplement. (2025, May 1). Strategic empathy as a key leadership skill in 2025? https://www.peoplement.dk/strategic-emapthy/
13. Edmondson, A. C. (2018). The fearless organization: Creating psychological safety in the workplace for learning, innovation, and growth. Wiley.
14. Cuddy, A. J. C., Kohut, M., & Neffinger, J. (2013). Connect, then lead. Harvard Business Review, 91(7–8), 54–61.

Chapter 3

1. Carreño, A. (2024). Leadership communication during organizational change. Journal of Information Systems and Engineering Management, 9(1), 45–68.
2. Edmondson, A. C. (2018). The fearless organization: Creating psychological safety in the workplace for learning, innovation, and growth. Wiley.
3. Pink, D. H. (2009). Drive: The surprising truth about what motivates us. Riverhead Books.
4. Quote Investigator. (2017, May 23). Culture eats strategy for breakfast. https://quoteinvestigator.com/2017/05/23/culture/
5. Gallup, Inc. (2024). State of the global workplace: 2024 report. Gallup Press. https://www.gallup.com/workplace/349484/state-of-the-global-workplace.aspx

6. Gallup, Inc. (2024). State of the global workplace: 2024 report. Gallup Press.

Part 2

1. Emerson, R. W. (n.d.). [Quote commonly attributed to Emerson]

Chapter 4

1. Edmondson, A. C. (2018). The fearless organization: Creating psychological safety in the workplace for learning, innovation, and growth. Wiley.
2. Siegel, D. J. (2007). The mindful brain: Reflection and attunement in the cultivation of well-being. W. W. Norton & Company.
3. Bar, M. (2007). The proactive brain: Using analogies and associations to generate predictions. Trends in Cognitive Sciences, 11(7), 280–289. https://doi.org/10.1016/j.tics.2007.05.005
4. Pelphrey, K. A., & Carter, E. J. (2008). Brain mechanisms for interpreting the actions of others in the social world: The role of the STS region. Trends in Cognitive Sciences, 12(3), 99–105. https://doi.org/10.1016/j.tics.2007.12.003
5. Duhigg, C. (2012). The power of habit: Why we do what we do in life and business. Random House.
6. Hatfield, E., Cacioppo, J. T., & Rapson, R. L. (1994). Emotional contagion. Cambridge University Press.
7. Kornell, N., & Finn, B. (2016). Feedback in learning. Current Opinion in Psychology, 9, 16–20. https://doi.org/10.1016/j.copsyc.2015.09.005
8. Cummings, T. G., & Worley, C. G. (2015). Essentials of organizational development and change (10th ed.). Cengage Learning.
9. Cummings, T. G., & Worley, C. G. (2015). Essentials of organizational development and change (10th ed.). Cengage Learning.
10. Edmondson, A. C. (2018). The fearless organization: Creating psychological safety in the workplace for learning, innovation, and growth. Wiley.

Chapter 5

1. Heath, C., & Heath, D. (2017). The power of moments: Why certain experiences have extraordinary impact. Simon & Schuster.
2. Damasio, A. R. (1994). Descartes' error: Emotion, reason, and the human brain. Putnam.
3. Goleman, D. (2013). The focused leader. Harvard Business Review, 91(12), 50–60.
4. Mehrabian, A. (1972). Nonverbal communication. Aldine-Atherton.

Chapter 6

1. Stone, D., Patton, B., & Heen, S. (2010). Difficult conversations: How to discuss what matters most (2nd ed.). Penguin Books.
2. Schein, E. H. (2017). Organizational culture and leadership (5th ed.). Wiley.
3. Schein, E. H. (2017). Organizational culture and leadership (5th ed.). Wiley.
4. Goleman, D. (2013). The focused leader. Harvard Business Review, 91(12), 50–60.
5. Schein, E. H. (2017). Organizational culture and leadership (5th ed.). Wiley.
6. Kahneman, D. (2011). Thinking, fast and slow. Farrar, Straus and Giroux.
7. Heifetz, R. A., Grashow, A., & Linsky, M. (2009). The practice of adaptive leadership: Tools and tactics for changing your organization and the world. Harvard Business Press.
8. Heifetz, R. A., Grashow, A., & Linsky, M. (2009). The practice of adaptive leadership: Tools and tactics for changing your organization and the world. Harvard Business Press.
9. Heifetz, R. A., Grashow, A., & Linsky, M. (2009). The practice of adaptive leadership: Tools and tactics for changing your organization and the world. Harvard Business Press.

Chapter 7

1. Goleman, D. (2013). The focused leader. Harvard Business Review, 91(12), 50–60.
2. Goleman, D. (2013). The focused leader. Harvard Business Review, 91(12), 50–60.
3. Goleman, D. (2013). The focused leader. Harvard Business Review, 91(12), 50–60.
4. Stone, D., Patton, B., & Heen, S. (2010). Difficult conversations: How to discuss what matters most (2nd ed.). Penguin Books.
5. McKee, A., Boyatzis, R., & Goleman, D. (2002). Primal leadership: Realizing the power of emotional intelligence. Harvard Business School Press.

Chapter 8

1. Goleman, D., Boyatzis, R., & McKee, A. (2002). Primal leadership: Realizing the power of emotional intelligence. Harvard Business School Press.
2. Castelo, S. L. (2024). The role of performance measurement and management in organizational performance. Public Money & Management, 44(3), 175–184. https://doi.org/10.1080/09540962.2023.2204400
3. Kaplan, R. S., & Norton, D. P. (1996). The balanced scorecard: Translating strategy into action. Harvard Business School Press.
4. Edmondson, A. C. (2018). The fearless organization: Creating psychological safety in the workplace for learning, innovation, and growth. Wiley.
5. Edmondson, A. C. (2018). The fearless organization: Creating psychological safety in the workplace for learning, innovation, and growth. Wiley.

Chapter 9

1. Collins, J. (2001). Good to great: Why some companies make the leap...and others don't. HarperBusiness.

2. Wiseman, L., & McKeown, G. (2010). Multipliers: How the best leaders make everyone smarter. HarperCollins.
3. Kegan, R., & Lahey, L. L. (2009). Immunity to change: How to overcome it and unlock the potential in yourself and your organization. Harvard Business Press.

Chapter 10

1. Kahneman, D. (2011). Thinking, fast and slow. Farrar, Straus and Giroux.
2. Dweck, C. S. (2006). Mindset: The new psychology of success. Random House.
3. Kock, F., Berbekova, A., & Assaker, G. (2019). Empathetic leadership: How leader emotional support and understanding foster performance. Journal of Leadership & Organizational
4. Studies, 26(2), 149–164. https://doi.org/10.1177/1548051819833378
5. Ickes, W. (Ed.). (1997). Empathic accuracy. Guilford Press.

Part 3

1. Greek proverb. (n.d.). A society grows great when old men plant trees whose shade they know they shall never sit in.

Chapter 11

1. Goleman, D. (1995). Emotional intelligence: Why it can matter more than IQ. Bantam Books.
2. Lencioni, P. (2002). The five dysfunctions of a team: A leadership fable. Jossey-Bass.
3. MindTools. (n.d.). 8 ways to resolve conflict in the workplace. Retrieved August 10, 2025, from https://www.mindtools.com/ahcpfn4/conflict-resolution
4. Stone, D., Patton, B., & Heen, S. (2010). Difficult conversations: How to discuss what matters most (2nd ed.). Penguin Books.

5. Vallette d'Osia, A. (2024). Empathy in the workplace: Disentangling affective from cognitive empathy. Journal of Work and Organizational Psychology, 8(2), 197–221. https://doi.org/10.1007/s41542-024-00197-9
6. Neck, C. P., & Manz, C. C. (1992). Thought self-leadership: The influence of self-talk and mental imagery on performance. Journal of Managerial Psychology, 7(6), 17–31. https://doi.org/10.1108/eb043409

Chapter 12

1. Mark, G. (2023). Attention span: A groundbreaking way to restore balance, happiness and productivity. Hanover Square Press.
2. Harvard Business School Online. (2019, November 14). 8 essential leadership communication skills. Retrieved August 10, 2025, from https://online.hbs.edu/blog/post/leadership-communication
3. Nowack, K., & Zak, P. (2020). Empathy enhancing antidotes for interpersonally toxic leaders. Consulting Psychology Journal.
4. Practice and Research, 72(3), 180–195. https://doi.org/10.1037/cpb0000168
5. Grimes, K., Demeke, B., Guay, A., Potvin, L., & Aubé, T. (2022). Leaders' role in building resilience and psychologically healthy workplaces. Healthcare Management Forum, 35(6), 306–310. https://doi.org/10.1177/08404704221157047
6. Kraemer, H. M. (2021, October 15). Leading is tough right now. But you've got this. Kellogg Insight. https://insight.kellogg.northwestern.edu/article/leadership-during-crises

Chapter 13

1. Morgan McKinley. (2025, February 12). What the data says: Is hybrid work the key to employee satisfaction? https://www.morganmckinley.com/au/article/what-data-says-hybrid-work-key-employee-satisfaction

2. Peoplement. (2025, May 1). Strategic empathy as a key leadership skill in 2025? https://www.peoplement.dk/strategic-emapthy/
3. Murray, D. (2025, March 5). How can leaders show empathy in remote and hybrid work environments? Speakers Associates. https://www.speakersassociates.com/how-can-leaders-demonstrate-empathy-in-remote-or-hybrid-work-environments/
4. Nguyen, C., Flower, T., Paredes, T., & Nagase, R. (2024). The curse of online miscommunication. Languaged Life, UCLA.
5. Asfahani, A. M. (2025). Navigating digital leadership: Unraveling the dynamics of remote work environments. TEM Journal, 14(1), 823–835. https://www.temjournal.com/content/141/TEMJournalFebruary2025_823_835.pdf
6. Horton International. (2024). The 5 pillars of remote leadership success. Horton Group. https://hortoninternational.com/the-5-pillars-of-remote-leadership-success
7. Johns, T. (2024). Building trust in remote leadership: The new currency of distributed work. Harvard Business Review, 102(5), 36–44.
8. Johns, T. (2024). Building trust in remote leadership: The new currency of distributed work. Harvard Business Review, 102(5), 36–44.
9. Zak, P. J. (2017). The neuroscience of trust. Harvard Business Review, 95(1), 84–90.
10. Doxatalent. (2025, May 13). Why fully remote teams win in 2025. https://doxatalent.com/resources/avoid-two-classes-of-employees/
11. Johns, T. (2024). Building trust in remote leadership: The new currency of distributed work. Harvard Business Review, 102(5), 36–44.
12. AltoPartners. (2025, January 23). Ask Alto: What is strategic empathy, and why is it a key leadership skill in 2025? https://altopartners.com/news/2025-ask-alto-what-is-strategic-empathy-and-why-is-it-a-key-leadership-skill-in-2025
13. Kock, F., Berbekova, A., & Assaker, G. (2025). Empathy in leadership: A systematic literature review on the effects and process of empathetic leadership. Journal of Business

Economics. Advance online publication. https://doi.org/10.1007/s11301-024-00472-7
14. Rogers, E. (2025, June 2). The enduring power of legacy leadership: 8 traits that define legacy-minded leaders. Emily Rogers Consulting + Coaching. https://emilyrogers.com/the-enduring-power-of-legacy-leadership-8-traits-that-define-legacy-minded-leaders/

Chapter 14

1. Anonymous. (n.d.). The ultimate test of leadership isn't what you achieve while you're present, but what continues to flourish in your absence.

Acknowledgments

A note about the conversations in these pages: I have taken considerable licence in recreating dialogue that occurred over months and years of mentoring relationships. Please forgive the compression of complex, evolving discussions into discrete moments of insight. Real transformation rarely happens in perfectly quotable exchanges - it emerges through countless small interactions, tentative experiments, and gradual realisations. I have condensed these extended journeys into focused narratives not to mislead, but to make the essential patterns visible and the underlying principles compelling. The insights are authentic, even if the conversations as presented are reconstructed for clarity and urgency.

This book exists because of the many leaders who showed me strategic empathy in action long before I had words for what they were doing. They wielded understanding as naturally as others wielded authority, creating spaces where people flourished without ever calling it a methodology.

To my colleagues who practiced strategic empathy unconsciously and intuitively every day: you were my teachers before you knew you were teaching. In staff meetings where you noticed the quiet voice that needed encouragement, in difficult conversations where you chose curiosity over judgment, in crisis moments where you remained present to both the human and the strategic dimensions - you demonstrated what transcendent leadership looks like in practice. Your examples became the foundation upon which every framework in this book was built.

To the people I mentored and coached, who taught me far more than I ever taught them: our conversations about your trials and triumphs revealed insights I could never have discovered alone. Your willingness to be vulnerable about your struggles, your courage to experiment with new approaches, and your honest feedback about what worked and what didn't shaped every principle in these pages. You showed me that strategic empathy isn't something you add to leadership - it's something you discover was already there, waiting to be understood and developed. Your growth became my education.

To Deborah Patterson, whose positive feedback came at moments when I most needed to believe this work mattered: your encouragement sustained me through the doubts that accompany any attempt to articulate something as nuanced as human understanding.

To Dr Sue North, whose critical eye challenged all my writing, and the assumptions I made: you sharpened my arguments and saved me from the comfortable imprecision that weakens so much writing about leadership. This book is stronger because you insisted it could be better.

To Allan Smith, who always had faith even when I didn't: your unwavering belief that I could do this sustained me through the moments when the gap between vision and reality felt insurmountable. When doubt crept in, your confidence reminded me that the most important revolutions begin with someone willing to believe in possibilities others can't yet see.

To Professor David Clarke at The University of Melbourne, whose voice I still hear in every sentence I write: you showed me that academic rigor and plain English are not opposing forces but natural allies. Your gift was taking ideas that hid behind jargon and freeing them into language anyone could grasp, without losing an ounce of their power or precision. You taught me that keeping a narrative alive and compelling isn't about sacrificing substance - it's about respecting readers enough to give them both clarity and depth. Five years after your passing, your influence remains woven through every page of this book. I hope these pages honour what you taught me: that the most important ideas should be accessible to everyone who needs them.

To my school leadership team, who taught me something new every day simply by being human beings navigating complex challenges: you were my laboratory for understanding how strategic empathy works in real time, under pressure, with real consequences. Your diverse perspectives, honest reactions, and willingness to engage in difficult conversations provided the raw material from which these insights emerged. You showed me that strategic empathy isn't a soft skill overlay but the foundation of everything that matters in leadership, even though I got it wrong so many times.

And to the leader whose story inspired this work but whose name I cannot share: your isolation taught me that even the most capable and confident people need connection, that authority without understanding becomes a burden too heavy for anyone to carry alone. Your memory reminds me why this revolution in leadership approach matters beyond theory or technique - it's about creating conditions where no leader suffers in silence, where understanding becomes as natural as breathing, where strategic empathy prevents the tragedies that happen when human beings are reduced to positions on organisational charts.

Finally, to every reader who recognises themselves in these pages and chooses to continue the conversation: you are not just learning about strategic empathy, you are becoming agents of its spread. The revolution described in these pages depends entirely on leaders like you who understand that the most strategic thing any of us can do is genuinely understand the people we serve.

The bridge has been built. The rest is up to you.

Made in United States
Cleveland, OH
07 December 2025